WHAT BIG GIRLS DO

The biography of Danielle King...
The ultimate true story of betrayal, survival, forgiveness, and healing

K.D.Kinz

What Big Girls Do
Copyright 2024 by K.D.Kinz
Published by Dreamflyer Publications

All rights reserved, printed in the United States of America. No part of this book may be used or reproduced in any manner whatsoever without written permission except for brief quotations embodied in critical articles or reviews. For permission requests, please contact the publisher at kdkinz414@gmail.com

Given the severity of the narrator's life story, the identities of certain persons, events, and communities involved have been altered. The author would like to stress that the narrator's real-life story is more traumatic than that presented in this manuscript. The author felt that only some details were needed to convey the story and message to the reader.

The following account is based on the true-life story of Danielle King. Names, locations, identifying characteristics, and some details have been partially altered, added, or withheld. Names, characters, businesses, organizations, places, events, and incidents are products of the author's imagination or are used fictitiously. Any supposed likeness to any persons, communities, or specific locations should be reconsidered, as some details have been modified. The story and dialogue have been reconstructed based on actual events, while others are reconstructed based on conversations, letters, photos, phone calls, police reports, and outcomes.

The author genuinely hopes that individuals will learn from this written work and go on to make the world a better and safer place, preventing such tragedies from happening in the future.

Any resemblance to actual persons, living or dead, events, or locales is coincidental. This book contains a mix of characters: some are inspired by real-life figures (in some instances, representing more than one individual); others are wholly imagined.

Original poetry by K.D.Kinz

https://www.facebook.com/what.big.girls.do/

kdkinz414@gmail.com
Library of Congress: TXu 2-455-470
ISBN: 9798328953948
Cover Illustration by Dreamflyer Publications © 2024
10 9 8 7 6 5 4 3 2 1

Danielle's Dedication

Dustin and Cassandra for everything

Terri (Gerry), Michelle (Jacques), Monique (Dan), and Tania (Chris), for lovingly guiding me back to the family and helping to prepare me for the next chapter of my life.

Uncle Camille, if you see my mother before I do, please tell her I love her.

K.D.Kinz's Dedication

Lyle and Erik, God bless you on your journey.

Thank you, Alpha & Beta Readers
V. Jean K.
Steve K.
Jess B.
Lois Z.
Kim. S.
Cheryl H.

Other books by K.D.Kinz:

Frogs In A Pot

After The We

Are You Dating A Narcissist?

In God, whose word I praise,
In God, I have put my trust;
I shall not be afraid.
What can [one] mere man do to me?

        Psalm 56:3

ONE

Manotick

1966

"**KAROLE AND DANIELLE**, get out of bed! We are leaving!" My mother urgently shook us by our shoulders in the middle of the night, her voice filled with a sense of impending necessity.

"I have school in the morning," I protested as I tried to reconcile the moment's urgency with the next day's routine.

"Where are we going, Ma?" my sister Karole asked, half asleep.

"Get out of bed and pack your clothes!" Mother switched on the bedroom light and swiftly snapped open our suitcases.

Karole and I didn't argue. The insistence in our mother's voice was unmistakable. We dragged ourselves out of bed and began packing our clothes. Moments later, Mother returned to our doorway.

"You don't have time to fold your clothes!" she exclaimed, as if folding was a mortal sin. "Throw them in the suitcase!"

I felt a rush of fear and uncertainty, my heart pounding in my throat. *Why are we leaving? Where are we going?* It felt like a nightmare I had experienced before.

Karole and I did as instructed and emptied our dresser drawers into our suitcases. Caniche, my stuffed poodle, was still lying on my pillow, where I had snuggled with her while I was sleeping. When I was four, I found her abandoned in a park near our home. We brought her home, and my mother washed her and sewed on new button eyes. I worked hard to squeeze her into my suitcase.

"Ma!" I cried out in panic. "I can't fit Caniche into my suitcase!"

"Leave it! It's just a stuffed animal!" Mother sternly yelled from the kitchen as she tossed pots and pans into a box.

"I *have* to take her with me!" My heart was pounding wildly, and tears ran down my cheeks... *Not again. This is not happening again.*

"Hurry up, girls! We have to leave… now!"

"May I take my spelling book along?" I loved school. I was learning to read, and I practiced my penmanship every day. I was proud of the homework assignment I would present to my second-grade teacher, Mrs. Kelson, in the morning. I had carefully printed each of my spelling words ten times over. I was certain she would smile when I submitted my spelling assignment—Mrs. Kelson had a gentle smile that I believed was meant just for me. No other grown-up had ever smiled at me that way, and I felt special in her eyes. I always did my best with homework assignments—my father would get upset if I brought home anything less than A's.

The other children in my class never expected to uproot and relocate to a new and unfamiliar city in the dead of the night. I treasured the one-room schoolhouse, knowing deep down that each day could be my last. My father could inform us at any moment that we had to leave.

"Danielle, pack your clothes and nothing more. We have no room for a stuffed animal or a school book! Now, hurry! Your father is waiting in the car!"

Karole's face tensed as she tried to carefully place her collection of waxed paper-pressed flowers into her suitcase—they were getting crushed. Our mother nervously entered the room again and saw what Karole was trying to do. She took the suitcase from Karole's hands, tossed the pages of pressed flowers to the floor, and snapped it shut. Then she took my suitcase from me as I was wasting precious time still trying to stuff Caniche inside.

"Karole, you can press new flowers in our next house. I'll buy a roll of waxed paper for you. Girls, you need to be brave! And stop crying!"

"Ma, we're in our pajamas. May we change our clothes?" Karole pleaded. It was the middle of a Canadian winter, and the car heater did not work well.

"We have to leave now! Don't you understand English?" she said in her French-Canadian accent. "Your father will leave without us if we aren't in the car within one minute!"

"I don't want Daddy to leave without me!" I cried through my tears. "Where are we going, Ma?"

"Danielle!" Mother snapped. I was making her angry with my persistence. "I'll explain later. Put your coats on!" She left our bedroom with our suitcases in hand, and Karole and I followed behind her like ducklings as we threw on our coats, hats, and mittens. She would never explain why we had to leave again—she never did.

At that age, I had already lived in various places but was too young to remember the specific locations. My memories from that time are hazy, but I recall the sense of urgency whenever it came time to leave. We spent weeks to months in each town before moving on to our next destination.

The house in Manotick had been my favorite. It was the town where I attended school and made friends. I especially liked Lester, my best friend. We played on the swings or teeter-totter during recess, and when recess was over, we held hands and skipped back into the schoolhouse. We were inseparable. Several times, we were reprimanded for talking too much, so we resorted to passing notes to each other when the teacher's back was turned.

I didn't understand why we kept moving to new places. I thought it was normal for families to do so until I heard other kids talk about growing up in the same town and knowing each other since they were babies. We lived in Manotick for two years, the longest we had ever stayed in one place. I hoped that our days of sudden relocation were over. After residing in Manotick, the memories of packing up and leaving town after town faded and were nearly forgotten.

With the moonlight guiding us, our mother opened the squeaky back door of our green sedan, and my sister and I climbed in.

"Theresa!" my father snapped at my mother. What the hell is taking you so long?!" He sat behind the car's wheel, the engine running, and a cigarette hanging from his lips. He was eager to leave.

"I'm sorry... The girls were moving slowly... And I had to pack up my kettles," she feebly explained.

Our heads flew back when our father pressed the gas pedal. He drove rapidly as if being chased, but no one followed us. In my seven-year-old mind, none of this made sense. I looked out the back window. Manotick grew further away, shrinking until it disappeared with my next blink.

We never questioned our parents' motives, but Manotick was the first town where we laid down roots, and this was the first time it physically hurt my heart to leave. *Is Caniche sad? Who will help Mrs. Kelson clean the erasers after school tomorrow? Would anyone find the spelling assignment I had placed on the dresser and give it to her?* Tears ran down my face. I didn't have the chance to bid farewell to Lester. How would he react tomorrow when my seat remained empty?

In the confusion of packing our suitcases, I slipped my First Place blue ribbon into my jacket pocket before leaving our bedroom for the last time. I treasured the ribbon, which symbolized the most significant achievement in my life: winning the spelling bee at the one-room schoolhouse. There would be consequences to face if my father found it. The name of our school was printed on it, and Mrs. Kelson had added my name with a magic marker. I kept my hand in my pocket and held it tightly. Feeling guilty, I retrieved it from my pocket and nudged Karole to show her what I had snuck out of the house. Her eyes widened in horror when she saw it.

"Throw it out," Karole mouthed as she pointed towards the window. I didn't want to throw my ribbon away, but was it worth the risk of being disciplined? I looked up at Karole, shook my head, and carefully placed the ribbon back in my jacket pocket.

"Daddy, where are we going?" Karole asked.

"Karole!" my father's temper surfaced. "I have to concentrate on driving, and you are a distraction! I don't want to hear one more word from either of you girls!"

Karole and I held each other's hand tightly to let one another know we were there for each other. I adored my big sister. My mother always seemed preoccupied, and I could never determine what consumed her thoughts. And while our father could be kind, he was short-tempered, and my stomach would knot whenever he was in a bad mood.

Karole always included me and brought me along on her adventures with the older neighborhood kids, even though I was fourteen months younger. Every day after school, we ran home to play with our friends. She was protective of me and never let any of the kids pick on me. She always had one eye on the game we were playing and the other eye on me.

Father favored Karole and wanted to make her strong like a boy. She was brave like he was, and she never showed weakness. I tried to be more like her so that my father would be proud of me, too, but time after time, I failed miserably. Sometimes, our father picked us up by our ponytails and swung us around.

Karole never cried. I tried to hold back my tears, but without fail, I would cry and beg him to put me down. I disappointed him. I was the weak one, and he reminded me of that daily.

Karole and I huddled under a blanket to keep warm. My father was driving at a more reasonable speed, and our initial frantic mood at the beginning of the trip diminished.

My mind drifted to the events of the past spring…

My grandfather died. My mother rarely insisted on anything, but she wanted to go to his funeral. My father was not thrilled with the idea of a twelve-hour drive to Hornepayne, but seeing how sad she was, he relented.

When we arrived, my grandmother hugged me. She gazed at my face with curiosity and smiled lovingly; it was our first meeting. I immediately wished our family could move into the house next door so I could visit her every day. Maybe we'd bake cookies and sit on the porch. It hurt my heart that I would only have her affection for a few days. We would drive back to Manotick, and I didn't know if I would ever see her again.

While sitting in front of the fireplace later that evening, my grandmother was shocked to discover that neither Karole nor I had been baptized. The following day, Grandmother called her parish priest, Father Johnson, to arrange for my sister and me to be baptized after our grandfather's funeral Mass on Sunday. Father Johnson wanted to take it a step further. One evening, he sat down with Karole and me at a table and taught us the Catholic Catechism in under four hours.

In addition to being baptized that Sunday, we received the Sacrament of Reconciliation and our First Holy Communion. I had never seen my mother so happy or my father so bored.

After the ceremony, I overheard Father Johnson talking to my mother.

"I don't understand, Theresa. You were raised in the Catholic faith. Why aren't you doing the same for your daughters?"

She responded in a quiet voice and then turned and walked away. Father Johnson's jaw dropped. It looked like he wanted to say more but was too shocked to speak.

"Ma, when are we going to go home?" Karole asked, snapping me out of my daydream. I couldn't believe she spoke up again. Our father had warned her not to be a distraction. He slammed on the brakes, tossed his cigarette out the window, and turned around to face us with fiery eyes.

"You two little brats better not ask any more stupid questions! The tractor belt is in the glove compartment, and I will use it!"

I thought my heart was going to pound out of my chest, but he did not get out of the car to whip our butts as I feared he might. Instead, he put both hands on the steering wheel, pressed hard on the gas pedal, and drove with determination. He had stopped the car to scare us, and it worked. We were saved from a licking because he was in a hurry to get us to wherever we were going. We would not say another word to our parents from that point forward unless spoken to.

Father would become furious at the slightest infraction. He especially got angry when my mother spent what he considered too much money. She had to account for every penny she spent at the grocery store.

But this time, my mother wasn't the person he was angry with. Somebody in Manotick must have done something to upset him, and I immediately wished ill upon whoever wronged him. There must be an evil person in Manotick, and he needed to get us out of town to keep us safe.

As the sun was rising, Karole and I remained as quiet as possible to hear anything our parents might say to each other. Our destination was being kept a secret, but eventually, we heard our mother say, "Calgary is over two thousand miles from Manotick." We could hear the crunch of the map as she studied it. She sounded stressed, and we were sure she didn't want to leave the house in Manotick. She had left behind beautiful furniture and the set of china that my grandmother gave her.

"Where is Calgary?" I whispered to Karole.

Karole started drawing a basic map of Canada in the condensation on the window. She had recently studied a map of Canada in school and had colored in all the provinces and territories for a homework assignment. She marked a dot on the far right of the window map.

"That's Manotick," she said under her breath. Then she made another dot on the left side of her map. "And that's Calgary," she added.

"Calgary is so far away from Manotick," I said softly, tracing the distance with my finger.

"It is… Calgary is all the way across Canada," she whispered back.

Hours later, we heard our father say something to our mother about "the bills." Karole and I concluded that maybe we had left Manotick because we didn't have enough money. *Maybe Daddy did not sell enough encyclopedias. Maybe bill collectors are chasing us. And maybe that is why he was driving so fast.*

We drove for days, stopping only for gas, to use the restroom, or to buy a loaf of bread and a package of bologna.

"Girls," my father barked into the back seat. "If someone asks you to tell them your last name, tell them you do not know."

My name was Danielle Bouchard… Why couldn't I tell anyone? Why was our identity to be kept a secret?

I trusted my parents implicitly. There had to be a good reason for uprooting us and leaving everything we owned behind in Manotick. I loved my parents and would be a good girl and not upset them by asking silly questions.

Caniche and Danielle (age 4)

TWO

My Mother's History

MY MOTHER, THERESA, was born in 1932 in Hornepayne, Ontario. She was the third of eleven children and the first girl in the family. Her parents (my grandparents) owned a grocery store and a bowling alley, and they were considered better off than most during the Depression. Theresa left school after the fifth grade to assist with household chores and care for her younger siblings. It was common for children to help during that time, as simple tasks like preparing daily meals could be complicated.

It wasn't all drudgery. She and her siblings played jokes on each other. Laughter was commonplace throughout the house, and her father may have been the biggest prankster in the family. Sometimes, when she told us about their pranks, Karole and I would laugh so hard that we could barely catch our breath.

As a teenager, Theresa worked as a waitress at a logging camp, skillfully carrying multiple plates and cups on her fingers to serve the hungry loggers. She must have been beautiful because, during that time, she received numerous offers for dates and several marriage proposals. Settling down was of no interest to the young Theresa, and she stayed focused on and loyal to her family, as they needed her.

The family often had an additional guest for dinner at their already crowded table. My mother's favorite guest was the parish priest, Father Johnson. The devout Catholic family of thirteen occupied an entire pew at Holy Name of Jesus Catholic Church every Sunday morning.

Of all the stories my mother told us about her childhood, one made an everlasting impression on me. The youngest of her siblings, Yvon, was conceived late in my grandmother's life and was different from the other children. Yvon was a good baby, always smiling. He didn't cry when he was hurt and didn't talk or walk until he was four years old. He was eventually diagnosed with Down syndrome, and my grandparents were told that he wouldn't live long. Amid their devastation, they turned to prayer, believing it was their only hope.

Meanwhile, everyone moved on with their lives... they had to. The doctors were correct in Yvon's diagnosis, but they were wrong in his prognosis, as Yvon thrived in his loving family.

To Karole and me, our mother had an idyllic childhood. She had parents who loved her very much and brothers and sisters with whom she could share her life.

Our mother told us she was not planning to marry at age twenty-four. She was happy staying home and helping her family. "Besides," she said, "who has time for dating when you have so much work to do?"

Mother told us about the day she met my father. She wasn't feeling well and was curled up in a big living room chair covered with a blanket when she heard a knock at the front door. Her older brother Peter answered. Two vacuum-cleaner salesmen stood outside the screen door while Peter went to find their parents.

Theresa peeked out from under her blanket, curious to see who the two strangers were. Quickly deciding that she had no interest in them, she laid her head back down on the arm of the chair. Then she heard one of the men say to the other, "She is beautiful, and she's going to be my wife someday." Theresa laughed to herself and thought, That is never going to happen. He is arrogant, and he's old enough to be my father.

The two men presented their pitch to Theresa's father, my grandfather, who rejected them and sent them away, making it clear that spending money on a fancy vacuum cleaner was out of the question.

The next day, the arrogant man returned and introduced himself to my grandfather as Jack Bouchard. He held a bouquet of red roses and asked permission to take Theresa out for ice cream. My grandfather was worried that Theresa was too attached to her family and that she might end up an old maid. Despite his concerns about Jack's age, my grandfather agreed, but Theresa's heart was not in it.

To please her father, Theresa stopped resisting the idea of marriage and began to dream of having a family of her own. They dated for a few months before Jack asked my grandfather for permission to

marry Theresa. Once again, my grandfather agreed—Jack was persuasive—but with the condition that Jack convert to Catholicism.

My mother often spoke about how diligently our father worked to convert to the Catholic faith. After receiving several months of instruction from Father Johnson, he was baptized on a summer afternoon. Our mother became convinced that Jack was the right man for her, despite their twenty-year age difference, after witnessing his dedication to their relationship. Her unwavering belief in a lifelong commitment to marriage between a man and a woman was guided by her faith.

My mother shared pictures from their wedding day. She looked beautiful as a bride, and my father was a handsome groom. However, I noticed she wasn't smiling in the photos, making me wonder if she had reconsidered marrying my father.

They spent their honeymoon at Niagara Falls. She described its beauty, and I pictured the romantic start to their new life in such a wonderful place. However, her life was about to change in ways she could not comprehend, and the pain in her eyes was evident as she told us about the chain of events that occurred after she married our father.

Mother explained that she had never been with another man before she married our father and did *not* enjoy her "wifely duties." Karole and I were too young to comprehend the significance of what she was telling us, but we nodded in complete agreement.

Months into their marriage, Theresa became pregnant with her first child. She described the labor as painful and prolonged. My sister was born weighing eight pounds, which was quite large for a petite woman to give birth to.

When my father discovered the baby was a girl, he felt disappointed; he had hoped for a boy. Five months later, my mother became pregnant with me, and my father accused her of cheating on him throughout her pregnancy.

When I was born, my father denied that I was his daughter. He was disappointed with the birth of a second girl and told the doctor to "put her back in." Shortly after I was born, my father underwent a vasectomy without discussing it with my mother beforehand, leaving her heartbroken, as she had wanted more children.

My sister and I used to hurry through our chores to join our mother at the kitchen table, sipping tea and listening to her stories of the past. My mother's eyes lit up when she talked about her family, and I could feel their love for each other. During these conversations, my father would be in the next room watching television, disinterested in what was happening at the kitchen table. He controlled what programs we watched on TV, so sitting at the wooden table with my mother was always the better option.

Karole and I felt immensely grown up during tea with our mother. She spoke to us almost as if we were her friends, not just children. We stirred heaping teaspoons of sugar into our tea and listened intently to every word she had to say.

During our discussions, my mother said, "Do not have children when you get married. They limit your choices in life. Stay single if possible. That way, you'll never have to answer to anyone." She also confessed to us that our father had been married previously and had not disclosed this to her before their marriage.

Some of her words were harsh, but she had no one else to confide in. Her siblings lived far away, and with her chores and her job, she had no time to form any meaningful friendships.

She shared how difficult it was to have two babies so close in age, one barely walking and the other in her arms. My father didn't provide any support when she needed it most. After I was born, my sister demanded attention and was unhappy if she didn't get it. On the other hand, I was a quiet toddler and would play with a shoebox for hours.

She explained that a woman should always look attractive to her husband when he comes home after a long workday.

"A wife should fix her hair, put on makeup, prepare dinner, and serve him promptly. And the Bible states, a woman should always submit to her husband."

Almost as if she were thinking aloud, she talked openly about how our family relocated every few months and how my father would give the family a new last name each time we moved. She explained that he would walk through a cemetery, choose a name from the headstone of someone around his age, and then use that name to obtain a new Social Security card. Karole and I never realized that his behavior was unusual. We just let our mother talk until she got everything off her chest.

THREE

Life Before Manotick

Somewhere in Virginia, 1960

WHEN I WAS two years old, we lived in a rented house in rural Virginia, and our nearest neighbor was over ten miles away.

My father would leave for weeks while traveling as a salesman. We survived on my mother's canned food, the bread she baked every morning, and vegetables straight from our garden during the growing season. During the frigid winter months, Mother gathered wood and kept the fireplace burning to prevent us from freezing to death.

Many poisonous snakes lived in Virginia, so Mother feared letting Karole and me play in the yard. She found an old lawnmower in a shed and started it. She then began mowing a patch of grass, hoping the snakes would stay away. Unfortunately, she ran over an old tin can, and the lid flew off, cutting her leg.

She had no phone, car, or way to get help. She managed to stop the bleeding, but she was afraid that she would die that day, leaving my sister and me alone.

One of my earliest memories is of my father walking into the house after being away for a long time. He held two puppies in each arm to solve the snake problem. We named the dogs Pat and Midge.

We left the Virginia house in the middle of the night during a thunderstorm. I remember whining as I climbed into the car that night.

"I don't want to sit by the hole!" A rusted-out hole on the car floor terrified me. I was afraid I'd fall through it. During the day, we could see the road rushing past the hole. If the road was wet and the car hit a bump, we got splashed with dirty rain or slush. Without complaining, Karole got in first and sat by the hole.

Every time my father drove over a puddle, Pat and Midge were splashed with mud through a hole in the station wagon's floor. My father stopped the car, let the dogs out, and continued driving. My mother adored those dogs, and tears filled her eyes each time she recalled that memory.

Quebec City, 1961

WHEN I WAS three years old, I developed a habit of sucking my fingers, which greatly upset my father. Despite all my mother's efforts, nothing worked to get me to stop. Although she never explicitly stated what my father did to me, I could tell from her expression that she disapproved of his method of discipline. She admitted, "I couldn't take it any longer... He was so hard on you."

In desperation, she consulted a doctor about the situation. The doctor informed her that she was on the verge of a nervous breakdown and suggested that she and my father give me up for adoption.

A decision was made: I would live with my mother's aunt. My mother packed my things and arranged to take me to her aunt's house. Her mind was made up—she had no other options.

That same evening, my father pleaded with her to give him another chance. He promised my mother that he would never again discipline me in that way. She relented and unpacked my things.

I never found out how he disciplined me, which upset my mother to the point that she felt she had no choice but to remove me from our family. As an adult, I considered asking her many times what he did to me, but then decided it wasn't worth upsetting her over something that occurred so long ago.

Somewhere in Vermont, 1963

OUR FAMILY MOVED to Vermont, where my parents began managing a campground. The campground had an office and a small grocery store. Every Friday, if my sister and I cleaned the bathrooms and shower stalls and picked up the campers' garbage, we were rewarded with a candy bar.

We lived in a house surrounded by swaying trees down the street from the campground. Gazing up at the trees, I was convinced the birds were singing only for me.

During that period, my father paid close attention to Karole's and my diet. As a skinny child, I found it challenging to chew meat during dinner. The more I chewed, the larger the gristle grew in my mouth. This upset my father so much that he spanked me after every meal until I stopped the habit.

If either Karole or I ate something that made us unwell, my father would disapprove and give us a spoon, insisting we eat whatever caused our sickness again. Whipped cream made Karole ill, while I had the same reaction to corned beef hash. He ordered our mother to keep serving us these dishes until we could eventually keep them down.

One morning, when we arrived at the campground, my father discovered the store had been broken into.

"Theresa, take the girls and get in the car," he said in a panic.

"Call the police, Jack," she replied.

"Don't be foolish," he scolded. "My fingerprints are all over this place."

My father drove us slowly out of the campground, ensuring we did not disturb the campers. Soon, the campers would wake up and head to the store to buy bacon and eggs for their breakfast or a float toy for the lake. They would take showers, use the bathrooms, and light campfires to make coffee. Driving away, I wondered who would be there to help them.

We hurried back into our house, quickly packed our clothes into suitcases, and returned to our car. After living for six months in the home surrounded by swaying trees, we left.

As we drove away, I felt numb. I found a bike a camper had left behind, a Barbie doll, and some Barbie clothes. But as the objects I possessed grew further and further behind while my father sped away, I felt nothing. The campers set up camp, and in a few days, they would be gone. I had played with a few girls my age but felt no sadness when they folded their tents and waved goodbye. I had no connections to things or people outside my family and no idea that life could be different.

Utah, 1964

WE DROVE FOR weeks. Karole held my hand while I quietly cried; I couldn't take it any longer. My sister and I were filthy from the dirt that flew through the hole in the floor whenever the car hit a puddle. Karole found a piece of cardboard at a rest stop and used it to cover the hole, but it only worked until it got wet.

As always, we listened closely to catch the slightest details about our destination that our parents might mention. We finally overheard them discussing Utah.

"Where is Utah?" Karole asked our mother while inside the Ladies' Room at a rest stop.

"It's on the western side of the United States. We will be there in a day or two." Our destination was once again on the opposite side of the country.

Our breakfast, lunch, and dinner consisted of bologna sandwiches. The sandwiches were easy to make, and my mother passed them back to us as we drove.

We spent several days driving around Utah as my parents looked for a place to live. They found a double-wide trailer with a "for rent" sign in the window. It was situated on a large piece of land and included a barn.

"This is perfect!" my father exclaimed. "I'm going to buy a horse!"

Shortly after we moved in, my father bought himself a buckskin horse. At six years old, the horse appeared enormous, and I feared he might step on me. Before long, my father brought home a second horse, a Shetland pony named Sissy. She was mean and bit my sister and me, and we suspected her aggression was the reason the owner gave her away.

My father bought a saddle at an auction for his horse. Several days later, the police came to our house and inquired about the saddle. The auctioneer was unaware that he had sold stolen goods. Cooperatively, my father entered the barn with the officers, and moments later, the police emerged, carrying the saddle. When my father returned to the house, he looked scared. He approached my mother in the kitchen as she prepared dinner.

"We're leaving when the sun goes down," he ordered. Karole immediately placed a finger to her lips, signaling for me to be silent so she could eavesdrop on their conversation.

"Why?" my mother replied in a nervous voice. "How could you have known the saddle was stolen when you bought it? This is not your fault!"

"Theresa, some monkey stole that saddle, and my fingerprints are all over it! We need to get the hell out of the States!"

Again, my father was concerned about his fingerprints, but his word was law. After living in the double-wide trailer for a year, we packed our clothes, left our toys behind, and let the horses free to fend for themselves. After sunset, my family was in the car, leaving Utah. I never liked Sissy the Shetland pony, but I hoped she would be okay with nobody to care for her.

"Why is Daddy always worried about his fingerprints?" I whispered to Karole as we drove away.

"I think he's afraid of policemen."

"Daddy is not afraid of anything!" I objected.

Manotick, 1964

WE SPENT DAYS on the road as our father crossed the country again. Karole and I often wondered why he always chose places so far away. We passed city after city, leaving them in our dust.

When we stopped for food or a bathroom break, he ordered us, "Don't talk to anyone!" I didn't understand why I could not talk to people, but I did as I was told. I wanted to smile at kids my age, but I knew he wouldn't want me to do that either. So, I looked straight ahead wherever I went and avoided eye contact.

A few days into our journey, our car broke down on the side of the road. Thankfully, a passerby stopped to assist us, attached our vehicle to his with a chain, and towed us to the nearest town. We spent that night in a motel; my father introduced himself to the check-in clerk as Mike Miller. I remember waiting impatiently for my turn to use the bathtub.

Our car was beyond repair, so my father bought a green sedan from a lot. I was not sad to see the station wagon with the hole in the floor left behind. I was clean from a bath I had taken the night before, and it looked like it was about to rain.

My father spoke to my sister and me as we stared mindlessly out the windows.

"Girls, we will be crossing the border into Canada shortly. When the crossing guard talks to me, stay under your blanket and pretend you are asleep. Do not say a word. If he does talk to you, your last name is Williams. Do you understand?"

"Yes, Daddy," Karole and I answered in unison.

"Karole… What is your full name?" Father sternly asked.

"My name is Karole Ann Williams," my sister answered succinctly without batting an eye.

"Danielle… What is your full name?"

"Danielle Theresa *Miller*!" I said proudly.

"What did you say?!" His voice felt like a lightning bolt that struck me directly in the stomach.

"Daddy," I started to cry. "Last night at the motel, you told the man your name was Mike Miller."

"Danielle, answer your father correctly!" my mother interjected, trying to prevent him from getting even angrier with me.

Karole leaned toward me and whispered in my ear, "Say, 'My name is Danielle Theresa *Williams*.'"

"My name is Danielle Theresa Williams!" I echoed loudly and clearly. My stomach hurt, and I doubled over from the pain. I felt like vomiting, but I managed to hold it back while Karole rubbed my back.

When we reached the border crossing, the sun was starting to rise. My father rolled down his window, and his demeanor changed when he locked eyes with the crossing guard. He spoke to the guard as if he were a long-lost friend.

"Hello, good sir," my father cheerfully said. "I'm taking my family to visit their sick grandmother."

Karole and I remained perfectly still under the blanket in the backseat, afraid to breathe. I heard my heart pounding in my ears. I was scared that the crossing guard would talk to me. "Danielle Theresa Williams, Danielle Theresa Williams, Danielle Theresa Williams," I whispered into my pillow.

"What is your destination, sir?" the guard asked.

"Montreal," my father lied.

"Okay!" the guard cheerfully said as he hit the top of our car with his hand. "Have a safe trip!" The guard never lifted the blanket to check on us. He never spoke to us, so for all he knew, we were two dead bodies.

Karole and I sat perfectly quiet for hours, listening to our parents' conversations. They spoke infrequently and then only about directions. Karole and I made eye contact when we thought we heard something important. To communicate secretly, we became proficient at reading each other's lips or writing words in each other's hands.

"Manotick is not too far," our mother said as she studied the map. "We should arrive in several hours."

"Girls, wake up! Look! That is the school you both will attend!"

My eyes widened as I focused on the one-room schoolhouse as we passed.

"Karole, you will go to second grade, and Danielle, you will go to first grade."

"Can we go to school tomorrow?" I asked, overly excited.

"We'll have to see. We need to find a house first."

It was the first time in a long while that I heard my mother sound happy.

FOUR

Calgary

1966 (continuation from Chapter 1)

MANOTICK WAS THOUSANDS of miles behind us. That morning, I accepted the harsh reality that I would never see Lester or step inside my school again.

My father took brief naps when we pulled over at a rest stop, while my mother didn't sleep for days. Every time I looked toward the front of the car, she was staring straight out the windshield.

"Where are we?" I asked nobody in particular as I rubbed the sleep from my eyes.

"We're in Calgary, Alberta," Mother said flatly. I struggled to discern whether she felt happy or disappointed.

My father spotted a motel on the side of the road, parked the car, and went inside. Minutes later, he was back with the room key.

"The rent is more than I wanted to pay for this dump." He was disgusted, but he was out of options.

Only one bed was in the motel room, so Karole and I made our bed on the floor. I didn't mind—after sleeping for days in a moving vehicle, I was grateful for a stationary place to rest. During the trip, I could only wash myself in rest-stop sinks, so I looked forward to my turn to use the bathtub.

I went outside and picked some flowers growing next to the building. I found a glass jar in a trash can that worked perfectly as a vase. I was hopeful that Karole would like the flowers and that Mother would soon go to the grocery store and buy waxed paper so Karole could press them.

"Danielle, get in here immediately!" my mother yelled out the motel room door. "Whatever are you doing?"

"I'm picking flowers for Karole," I said sheepishly as I realized I was doing something wrong.

"Don't be foolish, Danielle! We don't have wax paper or an iron. Get back in here and unpack your suitcase!"

Within a few days, my mother found a job at a bakery, and my father secured a position as a construction worker on the Crowchild Bridge.

While our parents were out all day, Karole and I were told to collect bottles and aluminum cans for recycling and return to the motel when the bags were packed.

After a couple of weeks, I had worn holes clear through the soles. As we ate our dinner that evening, I told my parents.

"Daddy and Ma, look…" I turned my foot to show my parents the bottoms of my shoes. "My shoes have holes in them."

"You should never have worn those shoes out so quickly!" my father scolded. He removed the tattered shoes from my feet and tossed them into the garbage can. "You will walk the rest of the summer barefoot, Danielle!"

Every day, Karole and I walked for miles on the hot paved roads, searching for bottles and cans. After a while, the calluses on my feet grew thick, and I no longer felt any pain. I did not complain, and I was proud in the evening when I returned to the motel room with my bag full of bottles and cans to present to my father.

Several months later, my father encountered a man at work who was looking for someone to live on his ranch for free, with the condition that the tenant complete a list of chores.

The weather was getting colder, and I was excited when my father gave my mother some money and instructed her to buy me a new pair of shoes to wear on the ranch. I promised to take good care of my new shoes—I never wanted to walk barefoot again.

FIVE

Calgary to Winnipeg

1966-67

THE HOUSE ON the ranch had no electricity or plumbing. The outhouse was filled with spiders in every corner, and the floor creaked under my slight weight. I was afraid of falling through the floor, landing in a pit of poop, and that nobody would hear my cries for help. I avoided the outhouse and often relieved myself behind a bush. Using the outhouse at night was terrifying, so I stopped drinking after dinner.

The house also didn't have a chimney, and at the innocent age of eight, I asked my mother, "How will Santa get in if there's no chimney for him to come down?"

Chickens freely roamed the property, and the owner left two dogs for us to take care of. Karole and I served the dogs a bowl of fresh water every morning and gave them each a scoop of dog food.

During the day, my father worked on the Crowchild Bridge while my mother, sister, and I cleared land from morning until late afternoon, stopping only to prepare dinner. The owner eventually informed us that we had cleared enough land, so our attention turned to the next task on his list: constructing a split-rail fence.

One evening, my father arrived home earlier than usual and called my mother inside. Karole and I overheard him yelling. He was upset about something that had happened at the Crowchild Bridge.

My mother told us to pack our suitcases. We knew the drill and precisely what was expected of us.

I was happy to leave the ranch—my mother, Karole, and I had worked hard during the six months we had lived there, and we were exhausted.

My father drove recklessly as if we were being chased. Realizing we would never receive an explanation, Karole and I again listened for details that shed light on our latest escape... A woman had accused him of something he didn't do. Someone had punched him, and in defense, my father punched him back. He justified his actions to my mother by saying, "I wasn't going to take it lying down. He had it coming."

My father was a powerful man. In his younger days, he earned awards for his strength, and I felt reassured by a father who could safeguard us from any danger.

Days later, we had driven across Canada, finally stopping when we reached Winnipeg. My father rented another motel room, and Karole and I helped our mother unpack and tried our best to make the room feel like home.

To break the monotony of living in a cramped motel room, my father would take the family to Victoria Beach. I remember feeling incredibly fortunate playing in the sand with my sister.

Weeks later, my father nervously announced that we were leaving. Something else had happened. My mother, sister, and I mechanically packed our suitcases and got into the car. We didn't ask any questions. We drove over two thousand miles, stopping only for gas, bathroom breaks, or to buy a loaf of bread and the usual package of bologna.

SIX

Ottawa

1967-68

WE DROVE FOR days, and we finally stopped in Ottawa. We lived in our car for weeks until our parents found a place for us to live.

The house they found would be the largest we had ever lived in, and we named it "The Big House." Karole and I couldn't wait to step inside. The previous renters had left furniture behind. The house had three bedrooms; this was the first time Karole and I wouldn't share a room. We wanted to move our beds into the same room, but our father forbade it, stating, "It's time for you two girls to grow up."

My sister and I had missed several school years, and I was getting worried. I knew catching up with kids my age would require a lot of work, and the problem grew as time passed.

"Ma, when will we go back to school?" I asked my mother as she prepared dinner.

"You will not be going to school," she sighed.

At that moment, my father walked into the house… He had heard the tail-end of our conversation.

"You are *not* going back to school!" he said gruffly.

"Why not Daddy?" I asked, knowing I was flirting with a whipping with the tractor belt.

"Because I said so! Do *not* question my authority!" he thundered. I bit my lip to stop it from trembling. I didn't want him to think I was weak. *He must have a good reason.*

Karole and I were prohibited from going outside or looking out the windows while our parents worked all day. We kept the curtains closed, which enabled us to move around the house freely, and we spoke in whispers to avoid being heard by the passing neighbors.

My mother got books from the library and told my sister and me that we should read them while she was away during the day. I had forgotten nearly everything I had learned in school.

Monday through Friday, Karole and I stayed in our room and studied. I don't know how, but we taught ourselves to read and write without a teacher or guidance. We played school, and Karole was the teacher. She would give me a page of arithmetic equations, and I did my best to solve them. Our mother could not help us; she read only French, as English was her second language.

We were permitted to play outside only after the neighborhood kids returned home from school, and we could blend seamlessly into a sea of children. Our mother instructed us… "If any children ask you where you go to school, change the subject."

On Christmas morning, there was a knock on our front door. My mother opened the door to find eight family members, each holding gifts and smiling. Tears ran down her face as she welcomed them in. Somehow, they found us and had driven twelve hours to surprise us.

Meeting some of my relatives for the first time made Christmas Day the most incredible day of my life. Aunt Noelle and Uncle George came, and I met my cousins Jon, Michelle, and Terri. The girls were near my age, and we instantly bonded. They asked me where my dolls were and seemed surprised when I told them I didn't have a doll. Instead, we got a deck of cards and played Rummy.

Clockwise (from top left):
Me, Karole, Terri, Jon, and Michelle, circa 1967

My grandmother seemed sad without my grandfather. I recalled how hard she and my mother had cried at my grandfather's funeral as they looked down at the casket.

The only thing my grandmother said to me that day was, "How is school, Danielle?" I wanted to tell her I had won the spelling bee two years ago when I went to school in Manotick. I wanted to tell her I was the best speller in the second-grade class and show her the "First Place" blue ribbon I kept under my mattress. Instead, I smiled and said what my father would want me to say.

"School is good, Grandmother." I felt terrible lying to my grandmother.

Uncle Yvon was there that day, and for some reason, it was decided that he and his Chihuahua would come live with us for a while. Several weeks later, he moved into our basement.

I loved the time Uncle Yvon lived with us. I had never met anyone like him before and quickly decided that people with Down syndrome were the kindest people on earth. Perhaps Down syndrome wasn't a disability—it was a gift. Uncle Yvon's positive outlook on life and genuine, cheerful attitude brought something to our family… a joy I never realized had been missing.

My mother decided we should start attending Sunday Mass at the local Catholic Church. My mother, Uncle Yvon, Karole, and I went for several weeks; my father refused to join us. Mother reminded us to wear a scarf. "Catholic women cover their heads in church in modesty."

My mother looked beautiful in her pink floral dress and lace scarf draped loosely over her head. I wore my favorite pale blue dress with a floral lace overlay—a hand-me-down from Karole. Karole wore a green daisy print empire-waist dress with long, puffy sleeves. We wore knee socks that matched our dresses and bobby-pinned scarves on our heads.

I held my mother's hand, and Karole held Uncle Yvon's as we strolled down the sidewalk to church. The summer sun embraced my face, and a gentle breeze lifted the scarf from my shoulders. At that moment, I was a princess walking with the queen. My mother explained to me that nuns were married to Jesus. I wanted to be married to Jesus. The church was a mile from our house, but I wished it were further... I didn't want the walk to end.

We sat in a pew toward the back of the church. During the Mass, my mind wandered as I glanced at other girls my age. They also wore pretty dresses, but their shoes were shiny patent leather with dainty straps. I tucked my feet under the pew to conceal my worn-out loafers—the only pair of shoes I owned.

After Mass, we were the first to leave. Our mother wanted to get home to our father as quickly as possible. It was time to make him dinner, and he would get angry if she served him late.

After attending church for several weeks, our father told us, "Going to Mass is a bad idea," and prohibited us from returning. I yearned to argue and express my love for wearing a pretty dress and sitting in Jesus's house. But I never dared to express those emotions; debating with my father was never an option... I would never prevail, and punishment would undoubtedly follow.

After a month, my father told Uncle Yvon that his dog barked too much and had worn out his welcome.

I didn't realize I could love anyone besides my mother, father, and sister, but I loved Uncle Yvon. I was devastated when my father spoke to him in that tone.

My father called Uncle Camille and yelled into the phone…

"You need to get Yvon and his dog out of my house! The dog barks constantly!"

Suddenly, he became quiet as he listened to Uncle Camille explain something. Then, in a nervous tone, my father asked several questions in quick succession: "How long ago were they there?" "What did they ask you?" "What the fuck did you tell them about me, Camille?!" The fact that someone was asking Uncle Camille questions about him made him exceptionally nervous.

He slammed the receiver down and yelled, "We're leaving! Pack up while I take Yvon to the bus station. Be ready to leave the minute I get back!"

Uncle Yvon seemed dejected as he got into the car, carrying his tiny dog in a metal crate. I thought my heart would break in two. It was as if my father couldn't get him out of our life fast enough.

I feared never again seeing my Uncle Yvon, grandmother, aunts, uncles, or cousins. My heart began to race as I watched my mother throw her kettles into a box, then run into her bedroom and pull our suitcases out of the closet.

She screamed in Karole's and my direction.

"Start packing! Take only what is necessary!"

"Ma, does Uncle Yvon know how to take the bus himself?" I was concerned. There were certain things with which Uncle Yvon needed help.

"He'll be fine. There will be people at the bus station to help him," she said, impatient with my question. "Start packing, Danielle!"

"Do our cousins know where we're going?" I innocently asked, fearing her answer.

"No."

"Can I send them a postcard, Ma?"

"No, you may not," she said sternly.

An hour later, my father returned. I walked outside to hand him my suitcase. Just then, a neighbor approached our driveway to investigate the commotion.

"You're leaving?" the neighbor asked.

"Yes." My father was annoyed. All he wanted to do was pack the car.

"Well, that is too bad. We never got to know you or your family. Say," the neighbor asked curiously. "Where do your girls go to school?"

My father paused momentarily as he arranged our belongings in the trunk and took a deep breath. "That is none of your goddamn business," he said as he slammed the car's trunk closed. The neighbor made eye contact with me as if trying to gauge whether I was okay.

Father spoke loudly as we drove away from The Big House.

"Karole and Danielle, in our next house, you will remain indoors unless accompanied by me or your mother! Do you understand?! I will not deal with nosy neighbors again!"

Was it all my fault? Did we have to leave because he was ashamed of me? *Does he have to hide me because he hates me?*

It was no secret that my father preferred Karole—even my mother admitted it. But if he hated me, why did he punish my mother and Karole, too? Maybe I was ugly. I already knew I was stupid.

I silently prayed as we sped out of Ottawa… *Please, Jesus, make me pretty and brave like Karole so Daddy will love me, too.*

SEVEN

My Father's History

MY FATHER, ALOUISE A. Parise, was born in 1912 in Vegreville, Alberta. He was the eldest of four children and the son of American citizens. "Jack" was the first name he used most often.

Throughout my life, I have encountered conflicting details about my father's life and attempted to unravel all the assumed names he used, only to discover yet another pseudonym whenever I think I have everything figured out.

My father was a human chameleon, constantly changing his identity as a way of life. The only consistent thing I remember about him is the cigarette that hung from his lips.

In stark contrast to my mother's childhood, my father told my sister and me stories of how difficult his childhood was. He told us that his mother disliked him… "She'd hang me by my thumbs and beat me." And while the rest of his family had steak for dinner, "I was given bread to sop up the grease left over in the frying pan." He never mentioned his father (my grandfather), so I always assumed my grandfather was a cowardly man who was submissive to his wife.

In his mother's opinion, his three sisters could do no wrong. He felt like a walking target—he was punished whenever his sisters were to blame.

My father's childhood stories were mainly dramatic, and I often felt that no one should have to endure the pain he went through as a child.

He shared anecdotes about unconventional pets like a bobcat and a moose and recounted a memorable tussle with a bear using his bare hands.

Like many young boys, Jack got into trouble. His mother punished him by ordering him to empty the backyard pond with a teaspoon and prohibited him from returning inside until it was fully drained. Realizing the futility of his task, he set the spoon aside and left home. He was thirteen years old at the time.

Eventually, he encountered Frank, who became his mentor and taught him vital skills such as hunting and fishing. Frank also taught him how to roll a cigarette. My father said living with Frank helped shape him into an upstanding citizen.

My father either dropped out of school after eighth grade or graduated high school in Tacoma. I've heard both versions but don't know which is true.

Young adulthood

WHEN JACK WAS young, he pursued a career as a professional boxer under the stage name Jimmy Britt. He was a fierce competitor and earned the nickname "Gentleman Jim" due to the respect he garnered in the boxing industry. He was five feet nine inches tall and solidly built. After breaking his hands and being forced to quit boxing, he transitioned to professional wrestling. He told my sister and me he had won the British Empire Light-Heavyweight wrestling title.

During our childhood, my sister and I witnessed his strength numerous times.

The War

MY FATHER TOLD my sister and me that he was in Canada on the first day World War II broke out in 1939. He proudly said, "Without hesitation, I enlisted in the Canadian Army and was on one of the first Canadian ships to land in Britain."

He also recounted the harrowing tale of the D-Day landing on Omaha Beach in Europe and the countless lives lost in the attempt to reach the shore. He served in the Canadian Army using the alias A. Alfred Aubin.

He told us he was quickly promoted from private to sergeant because of his quick wit and, "I took no nonsense from nobody." He admitted that he resolved issues with bulldog-like aggression, which resulted in time spent in "the clink."

Jack was injured during an attack in Britain. He said, "I took two machine-gun bullets home—one in my shoulder and the other in my thigh." He went to London to recover and was later sent to Iceland for light duty to complete his tour of duty.

Some of the stories he shared with us were difficult to hear. He mentioned, "Every man who went to war was left with deep scars in their hearts." When

Karole and I were young, he showed us the scars on his leg and shoulder from gunshot wounds.

After being injured, he returned to Canada and was assigned to an instructional training center because he was one of the three classified driver mechanics in the Canadian Forces. He continued working until his wounds healed and then resigned from the Canadian Army.

After returning from the war, he told us he wrote articles for a local newspaper about his experiences in the war.

In his mid-thirties, he started working in sales and claimed to be very successful. He said, "I had a sharp, sly tongue and could talk anyone into anything."

Growing up, I thought nothing about my father's life seemed easy. He was a fighter, and giving up was never an option or a choice he settled for.

He told us, "After the war, I met a woman and married her, but the marriage was short-lived."

He left out a few vital details.

EIGHT

Vancouver

1968-69

WE KEPT THE shades drawn in our apartment at all times. Karole and I were not permitted to leave, and we were not to look out the windows. We didn't exist in the outside world.

While we lived in that apartment, our father decided that we would speak French during dinner—speaking English was no longer permitted. Our family spoke only English while I was growing up, so speaking French proved challenging. I learned a few French phrases from my mother, but not enough to converse. Before every meal, Mother taught Karole and me the French words for each food we would be served. "S'il te plaît" and "merci" were my favorite words, and I said them with a perfect French accent, just like my mother. I don't recall how long our father insisted we speak French at the dinner table, but it seemed to go on forever. I suspect he made the rule so Karole and I would not talk much while we ate dinner.

Our father came home from work one day with an idea. If Karole and I could sing, we could become famous like the Jackson 5 or the Osmond Brothers. He called us out of our room and told us to sing for him.

Karole and I gazed at each other blankly. We seldom sang; we had little reason to.

"Daddy, should we sing in French or English?" Karole asked.

"Sing in English. Sing, 'You Are My Sunshine.'"

Karole and I opened our mouths and began to sing. However, as soon as we started, his forehead wrinkled, and he looked at us in disbelief. After the first verse, he held his hand up and instructed us to stop. His dream of having famous daughters ended as quickly as it had begun.

One morning, after my parents left for work, Karole didn't feel well. She lay on her bed, moaning as she held her stomach.

"Danielle, get a hot water bottle," she said as she rolled from one side to the other.

I went to the kitchen to prepare the water bottle when I heard a scream from the bathroom.

"Karole!" I yelled outside of the bathroom door. "What is wrong?"

"I'm dying," she said through the locked door.

"Karole, open the door!" I was frantic. If Karole were to die, I would certainly die, too. The door slowly opened.

"There is blood in my underwear," she said, embarrassed. "It's coming from my kiki."

Neither of us was aware of what was happening. For the rest of the day, I refreshed her hot water bottle and tried to get her to eat. She continued to rock back and forth as she held the hot water bottle tight against her stomach. I felt helpless; nothing I did helped, and she couldn't stop the bleeding. Hours later, my mother returned, and I ran to the door to tell her what was happening.

"Ma! Karole has blood coming from her kiki!"

My mother pushed past me, swearing a blue streak in her native tongue. She went straight to our bedroom and sat down next to Karole.

"Oh, my sweet girl," she stroked Karole's head. "You are not dying. You are becoming a woman. I told you that this would happen. Don't you remember?"

"But I don't want to be a woman!" Karole half-cried.

"Menstruation is a normal part of growing up, Karole. All women go through it. Without it, you wouldn't have babies."

"I don't want a baby!" Karole nearly screamed.

"Karole, your body is changing. You're starting to look more like a woman than a little girl. There is nothing to be afraid of," my mother said softly.

Earlier, I had found rags to shove between Karole's legs. Mother took Karole's hand and walked her into the bathroom.

"These are the pads that I use. You will have to change them every hour or two."

After I had spent the entire day in a state of panic, convinced that my sister was dying, my mother's kind words reassured me that everything was all right.

"Does Karole have to do this forever, Ma?" I asked.

"This will happen for a few days every month."

"Every month!" I was horrified. "Does this happen to you, too, Ma?"

"Yes, and it will happen to you, too, when you are as old as Karole."

"Then, I want to stay little forever," I firmly resolved.

Karole was beginning to seem more mature. She wore loose shirts to hide her breasts and requested privacy during baths. Up until that time, we had taken baths together. Sometimes, Ma would add bubbles to the water, and we would have fun making silly hairstyles and beards with the bubbles.

During this time, our father started taking Karole on business trips. However, she wouldn't accompany him when she was on her period because she experienced cramps and felt unwell. My father and Karole could be away for days, leaving my mother and me at home.

I envied the attention Karole got from our father, but I also cherished the quality time with my mother. My mother sensed I was unhappy and did her best to make our alone time memorable. We baked unique desserts and went on evening walks. And without my father to monitor the television, we watched whatever shows we wanted.

When my father and Karole returned from their business trips, Karole would show my mother and me the gifts my father had purchased for her. She had new dresses, purses, shoes, and jewelry.

When my father was out of earshot, my mother scolded Karole.

"How dare you flaunt your gifts, Karole! You are making your sister very sad! Stop encouraging your father to buy you all of these things! We can't afford it!"

The burden of my mother's anger toward my sister was heavy. Karole should have resented me for the pain I caused her... but she never did. It was quite the opposite.

Karole gazed at my mother wide-eyed and puzzled as if struggling to find the right words to respond to her.

For the first time, I resented Karole. I always knew our father preferred her over me, and I learned to live with that. But now, he treated her like a princess; his face lit up whenever she entered a room.

Karole couldn't have done anything to stop my father's overt affection or change the situation, but at the time, I was sure she could have. After he kissed her goodnight, rubbed her back, and whispered in her ear, she should have told him to kiss me goodnight, too. But she didn't, and I was upset that she kept all of his love and attention for herself. *She should share Daddy's love with me.*

NINE

Coquitlam

1969

WE MOVED TO a better apartment, a short drive from our last one. Karole and I remained hidden during school hours as in the previous apartment, and the blinds stayed drawn. We were only allowed to leave the apartment if one of our parents accompanied us.

We had no friends and did not associate with neighbors. Occasionally, when someone came to the door, my mother would be a basket case, worrying about us making noise in our room; we had to remain silent.

Now and then, I disobeyed my parents' orders and peeked through a crack in the blinds. The crack was already there, so I didn't think I was doing anything wrong. I watched as kids my age walked to school, holding books in their arms. The boys walked behind the girls, and sometimes the girls would giggle.

When Karole was with my father on a business trip and my mother left for work, I was alone, with only my books to keep me company. I devoured the books my mother brought home, especially the storybooks. I wasn't interested in the math books—I would much rather curl up in a chair and read *Little Women* from cover to cover. In that way, I escaped any self-pity I may have felt by reading about the hardships of Jo, Beth, and Amy.

In the quiet evenings, when it was just my mother and me, she taught me how to count change. I became skilled at it, and learning from my mother was much more enjoyable than trying to learn from a textbook. She also took me to the bakery where she worked and taught me how to cut bread for the customers.

If customers asked me a question, my mother was always nearby to rescue me from their curiosity. I was not to tell anyone I didn't attend school, and sometimes, our most recent surname didn't easily roll off my tongue. I didn't want to answer their questions incorrectly and get my mother in trouble, so I smiled and politely said only, "Thank you" or "Merci" when handing them their loaf of bread.

Karole still returned home from the business trip with gifts my father had bought her. However, she no longer showed them to my mother or me. Instead, when she arrived home, she quietly walked into our room and promptly put the gifts away in a dresser drawer.

I was thrilled when our father informed us it was time to leave Coquitlam. Living in an apartment with minimal sunlight and little contact with the outside world often put me in a bad mood. He said he found a two-story house on Vancouver Island. We quickly packed our suitcases. My sister and I couldn't imagine anything more exciting than living on an island in a two-story house!

We crossed the Strait of Georgia on the ferryboat. All of our belongings were packed into the trunk of our father's new Cadillac. At that moment, I felt blessed. *How many kids my age see all the places I've seen? How many kids get to travel as much as I have?* I didn't attend school, but maybe this was better. Maybe my parents knew that this was the best way to educate us. We didn't have to read about things—we experienced them firsthand.

TEN

Vancouver Island

1970

WHEN WE SAW the children returning home from school, Karole and I ran out the front door, jumped on our banana seat bikes, and rode straight to the beach. Despite having some freedom on the island, we were strictly instructed not to reveal any personal information.

By then, I had accepted our way of life and didn't realize it was unusual. I no longer asked my mother if I could go back to school. Karole and I spent our days reading books and doing chores. There was always laundry and cleaning, and now that we were older, we started cooking dinner so our mother didn't have to do it when she came home exhausted from work.

We got a dog named Bruce, and Karole and I were responsible for caring for him. We gave him a scoop of food in the morning and another before dinner. One day, in our rush to go to the beach, we forgot to feed the dog his second scoop of food. When we walked in the door at dinnertime, our father informed us...

"If you girls cannot remember to feed the dog, you won't be fed either."

Karole and I went to bed hungry that night. His harsh punishment taught us a valuable lesson; from that day on, we remembered to feed the dog.

Our mother sewed each of us a swimsuit that summer. Karole's was a two-piece heart print, and mine was a one-piece paisley print. Karole looked older than thirteen, and her curves were evident in her new swimsuit.

One weekend, my parents came to the beach with us. The four of us walked along the pier, passing by some fishermen, when suddenly, my father pushed Karole off the dock. I dashed to the edge to see if she was all right. I felt a shove from behind. I heard my mother scream, and I plunged like a rock into the water.

I sank deep down into the lake. Panicked, I prayed for my feet to touch something solid from which to push myself up. I attempted to slow my descent by wildly flapping my limbs.

At last, my face surfaced, and I gasped for air. Unfortunately, I also gulped down a lot of water. While still choking, I went under again. I held my breath, fighting the urge to cough. I kicked my feet and flapped my arms for all I was worth. I repeated the scenario countless times until I was sure that I was going to die.

Suddenly, I felt a firm hand on my arm, pulling me to the surface. My father dragged me by the arm to the beach, where Karole was already sitting on the sand, shivering under a beach towel. My mother reached out to me.

That's how my father taught us to swim.

Karole and I spent every moment possible on the beach that summer, but we never went into the water again. We met kids our age, told them our names were Marsha and Jan, and said we went to a private school twenty miles away.

The boys were drawn to my sister and ignored me. One evening, I spotted Karole kissing a boy behind the concession stand.

"Karole! What are you doing?" She looked at me with daggers in her eyes. "It's time to go home!"

I'm sure that I was very annoying. Although she was only a year older than me, she was so much more sophisticated.

"That's my boyfriend!" She informed me as we walked toward our bikes.

"A boyfriend? Why do you need a boyfriend?"

"Danielle! Honestly, you are such a child!"

We got on our bikes and headed home. The sun was starting to set.

We didn't attend church anymore, but it didn't matter. When my sister left on a business trip with my father, my mother talked to me about Jesus and the Ten Commandments. Every night, she sat at the side of my bed and recited the prayer, "Now I lay me down to sleep," before she turned out the lights.

I prayed constantly... I prayed that I wouldn't fall off my bike when riding as fast as my feet could pedal. I prayed for my family's well-being. I prayed for my father to love me as much as he loved Karole and asked Jesus to let us live on the island forever.

ELEVEN

Surrey

1970

AS WE DREW across the ferry to the mainland, I felt a tug on my heart. I could still hear the ocean waves and feel the ocean breeze in my hair as I rode my banana seat bicycle home in the evening as the sun dropped below the horizon.

I couldn't understand why we had to leave the island. One morning, with no warning, we packed up and left. My mother's expression was blank on the day we departed, and I could tell her heart wasn't in this move—but it hadn't been in any of our previous moves, either. We settled into an old ranch-style house.

A few days later, my father caught Karole smoking a cigarette on the side of the house. He took her into the living room, handed her a new pack of cigarettes, and ordered her to smoke the entire pack.

I watched out of the corner of my eye as my defiant, fifteen-year-old sister lit one cigarette after the other. About thirty minutes later, she looked green. I ran to get a bucket and took it to her.

"She can't smoke any more cigarettes, Daddy! She's sick!" I said. I couldn't tolerate seeing my sister so sick. She looked as if she were going to die.

My father casually walked over to me and slapped me across the face. "Never question my authority!"

Later that day, Karole finished the pack, went to our bedroom, and stayed in bed for two days. My father instructed me to stay away from her and said if he saw me bringing her anything, I would suffer the same fate.

I made a friend, Sue Ann. On weekends, she invited me to sleep over at her home. We had a great time making popcorn and watching movies in our pajamas. Sue Ann's parents took me under their wing and showed interest in my life.

One day, Sue Ann's father asked my father, "Why isn't Danielle in school?"

We quietly left Surrey that night.

TWELVE

Athabaska

1971-72

WE DROVE NORTH for days, and I was sure that my father had no idea where we were going this time. We stopped when we reached Athabaska, Alberta, then drove around for several more days to find a place to live. Karole and I overheard our father telling our mother that he had saved some money and that we could buy a place this time instead of renting.

We arrived at a run-down farm with a "For Sale: Farm on 180 Acres" sign in the front yard. My father had a plan...

"We can turn this farm into a hunting camp. I'll be the outfitter and take hunters to their campsite where they can hunt for moose. There is big game in this part of the country! Karole and Danielle, you will be wranglers!"

"What does a wrangler do, Daddy?" I asked.

"A wrangler is a person who takes care of the livestock."

I was thirteen years old, and being a wrangler seemed much more exciting than any other life I could imagine. However, the farm had been neglected, and it would take months or years to bring my father's vision to life.

"And Theresa, you will cook for the men." My mother didn't respond, and in his excitement, he failed to notice her total lack of interest.

We got out of the car and approached the front door. The lock was broken, so we walked in. The house was tiny and dark—the light switches were useless since the power was off.

In the kitchen was a yellow chrome table and chairs with torn seats that had been patched multiple times with duct tape, and the Kelvinator refrigerator was moldy inside. Our father said the appliances ran on propane and went outside to check the propane tank. When he returned, he extinguished his cigarette and took a matchbook from his pocket.

"Stand back," he said in a severe tone. Karole and I quickly left the house and fearfully watched him through the door. After swearing a blue streak at the old appliance, he successfully started one of the burners.

"It works, Theresa!" he proudly announced. My mother could have been more impressed.

"Daddy, there's only one bedroom. Where will Karole and I sleep?" I asked.

"We will build an addition to the house. It would do you girls a world of good to learn how to swing a hammer."

Our next stop was back in town to find a phone booth. I watched my father dial the number on the "For Sale" sign and then scribble in a notepad.

When he returned to the car, he told my mother, "The bank is a mile down the road."

Karole and I sat on the car's hood while our parents entered the bank to discuss the transaction.

"We're going to have a place of our own, Karole! We won't have to move anymore!"

Karole half-smiled. I wanted her to share my enthusiasm, but she wasn't the same as when she was younger. She didn't laugh much anymore. My mother said, "She is going through puberty, and sometimes girls get moody." I couldn't wait for puberty to be over.

We moved into our new house several weeks after closing the deal. My father told us he was planning to buy horses, and Karole and I would be responsible for caring for them because that's what wranglers do. He informed us that horses eat grass and hay, and Karole and I would need to shovel the horse manure every morning. We were excited despite not knowing precisely what manure was.

Early the next day, our mother woke us up at 4 a.m.

"Ma, it's still dark out!" Karole whined.

"You need to get an early start. Daddy left to find work. After breakfast, you two girls need to clean out the barn."

"I thought Daddy was going to be an outfitter!" Karole exclaimed. "And we are going to be wranglers!"

"I'm afraid that won't happen until after this place is repaired. We have a lot of work to do! Your father needs to work to pay our bills!" she said, shaking her head at her daughters' naivety.

When Karole and I swung the barn doors open, we were amazed to find it filled with rusty old farm equipment and miscellaneous junk. We spent weeks sorting and creating separate piles: one for old metal and one for usable items. We kept a fire burning and fed it for days with garbage the previous owners left behind.

We cleaned the stalls and old tin troughs, preparing them for our future horses. We brought several hay bales into the stalls and spread them out to make a bed for our future horses to sleep on.

We assisted our mother in planting a vegetable garden early in the growing season. She would have to purchase canning supplies and prepare for the upcoming winter. If we didn't get enough rain, it was Karole's and my job to haul buckets of water for the garden. The rabbits ate much of what we planted that season until my sister and I put a fence around it. Sometimes, our father shot the rabbits, and we ate them for dinner.

In early fall, my father started building an addition to the house. Karole and I assisted with sawing boards and pounding nails, and in under a week, our new bedroom was finished.

My sister and I had found an old metal frame bed in the barn, and we set it up in our new room. We didn't own a mattress, so we added blankets to the springs for padding. It creaked loudly when we sat on it, and I could still feel the metal springs through the layers of blankets. But it was ours, and I was not about to complain.

Mother had been canning vegetables for days and needed access to the cellar.

"Girls, open the cellar doors and clean it out. Then, I'll need your help moving the jars into it."

A foul smell hit us as soon as we lifted the cellar doors. Something had been living down there, and even Karole wasn't brave enough to climb the ladder to see what it was. We left the doors open for a few hours to let the critter out, but the stench lingered when we returned. Karole gathered her courage and started climbing into the cellar, holding her breath.

"There's poop down here! Lots of it!" she yelled up to me. Just then, she let out a blood-curdling scream. I froze, not knowing if I should go down to help her or run for my life. She quickly climbed back out.

"There is something down there! I saw it move!" She looked horrified.

"What is it?" I asked.

"I don't know, Danielle. Climb down the ladder and look for yourself!"

"Is it big?"

"Yes, it's big!"

"Is it a bear? I'm not going down there! Bears are mean!" I cried. "You are the brave one!"

"I'm tired of being the brave one," she said half-heartedly.

"Let's smoke him out!" I yelled. It was the best idea I could come up with.

"And burn down the house? Daddy will kill us both!"

At that moment, a neighbor's dog came sniffing and caught the animal's scent in the cellar. He started barking into the cellar; the hair on his neck stood up. Suddenly, a porcupine emerged from under the house, and the dog took off in hot pursuit. Karole climbed down again and informed me that the coast was clear. We spent that day shoveling out the cellar and wiping down the shelves. We used rocks to block the hole the porcupine had used as its entry point.

My mother obtained schoolbooks for us to read in the evenings. The books were tattered and worn, and I suspected she got hand-me-downs from a local school. Karole and I attempted to read and study whenever we had the time. I could read for about thirty minutes every evening, but I often fell asleep mid-sentence due to exhaustion from the day's work.

Karole and me

Our next task was installing electric fences for the horses my father planned to buy. After the fences were installed, the horses trickled in, one after another, and within a year, we had twenty!

Karole and I wake up at 4 a.m. every morning to feed and water the horses. We check the fences daily for needed repairs, as losing a horse through a breach in the wall would be catastrophic and result in punishment.

My sister and I were responsible for cutting down trees and storing wood for the winter. We found a bucksaw in the barn and quickly became proficient at cutting through trees. As a result, we had a large pile of dry wood and another pile of green wood that needed to cure for the following winter.

During this time, I started noticing changes in my body similar to Karole's, not just in building muscle. We had matured into shapely, young women, and we often found it amusing that our menstrual cycles synchronized. But there was no time to laze around and nurse our cramps. It was a luxury we could never afford, so we continued with our chores as we did every other day.

Our parents planned a two-week trip to Hawaii. My mother was unhappy about leaving two young teens without a phone or electricity, but my father was determined to go.

Before leaving, our father told us, "Move the hay pile ten feet to the left while I'm gone."

We were already overwhelmed with caring for the horses and all our other chores, and we had no idea why he wanted this done. However, we knew that if we didn't complete our assigned task, we would feel the sting of the tractor belt he kept on a nail in the kitchen.

We were two strong girls, but he was a formidable man. We would never challenge him. If we deserved a whipping, we accepted the consequences. He often reminded us of his days as a professional boxer, and we were confident he could still win a boxing match if given the chance.

Karole and I couldn't think of any logical reason to spend hours every day moving a giant pile of hay ten feet over for two weeks, except that our father wanted to keep us occupied in his absence. What did he think we were going to do? Go into town and meet people our age? Make some friends? Have a little fun? The town was miles away, and we had no transportation. Even if Karole was allowed to drive, our parents had the family's only car.

After two weeks, our parents returned home. Father immediately walked into the barn, glanced at the rearranged pile of hay, and left satisfied that we had done as we were told. As our reward, my father got two husky puppies, one for each of us. I named my dog Gypsy, and Karole named her dog Moses.

"The dogs are for hauling wood; they are not house pets," he firmly informed us. He showed us how to harness the dogs, which seemed cruel, but he assured us that the breed was created to be working dogs.

A year later, the business was booming with a constant flow of hunters setting up camps, and gunshots were heard throughout the day.

One day, a hunter commented to my father about how hard he saw my sister and me working. Knowing that money was no object for this particular man, my father saw an opportunity and seized it.

"My daughters can lift that freezer packed with meat," he said, pointing to a large freezer in the corner of a shed.

"I bet one hundred dollars that they can't!" the man retorted. "That's impossible!"

"Hey, I bet you five hundred dollars that they can lift that freezer!"

The hunter walked to the freezer, opened it, and found it packed with meat. He tried to push it, but it wouldn't budge.

"You're on!" the hunter said, shaking my father's hand.

Karole and I locked eyes. Neither of us knew if we could lift the freezer, but nothing much scared us anymore. We barely flinched when a moose jumped over the fence into our horse corral, and we didn't panic when we saw a grizzly bear walking on our property.

Karole got on one side of the freezer, and I got on the other. If we didn't lift it, our father would be angry. We had to lift it; we had no choice. We were strong girls. Our arms bulged with muscles from throwing fifty-pound hay bales every morning for the horses.

My father called me stupid and weak every day of my life. If I could lift this freezer, maybe he'd never call me weak again. *God, please help me.* Suddenly, I felt superhuman strength—the kind of strength you hear about in stories where a mother lifts a car off her child.

We both grabbed hold and lifted with all our might. The initial attempt failed, and I heard the hunter laugh.

"Wait!" Karole yelled firmly. My father and the hunter didn't dare move.

We grabbed hold once more… and lifted the freezer an inch off the floor.

The hunter paid up, and my father was ecstatic. I felt that I had earned a bit of respect from my father after proving my strength, but if I impressed him, he didn't mention it. He turned and headed for the house, counting his winnings as he walked.

Karole and I sat on the living room couch that evening, watching TV while our mother picked vegetables in the garden. Our father walked into the living room and began to undress. He removed his shirt, tossed it on a chair, then sat down and took off his shoes and socks. He stood up and removed his belt, unzipped his pants, and slid them off. I held my breath, horrified that he was undressing in front of us. Karole kept staring at the TV as if nothing unusual was happening. He then pulled down his underwear and stood naked just feet away from us. I kept my eyes on the TV and pretended I didn't notice. I had never seen a naked man before.

"You should know what it looks like," he said matter-of-factly as if he needed to educate us about the male anatomy. He seemed irritated that I did not look in his direction when he spoke. He picked up his clothes from the floor and casually walked through the room.

This was the first time he appeared naked in front of me, but it would not be the last. Seeing him walk through the house without clothes became a daily occurrence.

My father told us that we needed to finish our chores early that day because we were going for a drive to visit a friend named Jeannie, whom he had never mentioned before. He didn't provide any other details about their relationship, but Karole and I looked forward to a break from our chores and enjoying the scenery for several hours.

Jeannie, in her early twenties, greeted my parents with a half-smile when she opened the door. She was holding a toddler in one hand and balancing a baby on her opposite hip. She looked nervous as she listened to my father speak. Karole and I were playing with Jeannie's dog on the front lawn; it had bolted out the door when she opened it. We couldn't hear my father's words; he spoke quietly. Their conversation seemed pleasant initially, but within minutes, my parents walked briskly toward the car.

"We're leaving!" my father said sternly. "She is rude!" he yelled loudly. I was glad Jeannie had closed the door and likely didn't hear him.

During the ride home, the visit with Jeannie was not discussed, and "his friend" Jeannie was never referred to again.

That winter, my father bought a Ski-Doo snowmobile. My mother, Karole, and I watched him slide it off the trailer and start it up for the first time. He quickly made several laps around the property. Several horses whinnied inside the barn; they didn't like the unfamiliar sound of the snowmobile. He then drove onto a small, frozen creek that ran through our property. The days and nights had been frigid, and the ice was thick. As he approached the bridge that crossed over the creek, he slowed down and ducked to go underneath it. At that moment, the ice broke, and the machine fell through. The three of us started running in his direction.

"Daddy!" I screamed. I hoped we could reach him in time to help, but we still had a long distance to run. The creek was only a few feet deep, so I wasn't worried about him drowning. As we got closer, we watched in astonishment as he lifted the snowmobile onto the bridge.

"Oh, Daddy!" I cried. "You are the strongest man in the world!" He was strong, more powerful than any man I had ever known. How many girls could say their father is so strong that he can lift a snowmobile?

During Alberta's winters, temperatures often dropped well below zero. I vividly recall when it was sixty degrees below, and the snow was so deep that we were housebound for days. Gypsy and Moses enjoyed the snow while we shoveled a path to the barn to care for the horses. During the cold weather, we had to remove the ice from the horses' nostrils multiple times a day so they could breathe more easily.

Karole and I knew our responsibilities. We woke at 4 a.m. every morning and braved the elements to tend to the horses. We returned to the house by 6 a.m. for breakfast, which always consisted of oatmeal and toast. While my father ate bacon and eggs or pork chops and pancakes, he told us that his food was not good for us. It was a rare treat for Karole and me to eat those things. We worked as hard as any man and had appetites to match. We were always hungry, so we filled our stomachs and snuck food whenever possible.

I was a wrangler, and I was proud of myself. I no longer lamented the lack of an education. No other girl could do what I could do, and that was all that mattered to me.

When it got too cold for hunting, my father started a business selling smiley-faced, frown-faced, and buttons that said, "shit." He placed large orders, and my mother, Karole, and I worked all day and night to assemble the buttons and pack barrels for shipment to stores. After finishing the buttons, we still had the farm chores to complete

We had lived on the farm for two years. The business was doing very well, and I suspected my father was making a fair amount of money. But as hard as I tried, I could never make my father love me as he loved Karole. She was his favorite, and it was something I had learned to live with. Maybe he did believe that my mother had an affair and that I was not his daughter.

Karole was his chosen companion to help set up tents for the hunters; they could be gone for hours while setting up a new camp. Karole was also the only one he would take with him when he drove into town. To cheer me up, my mother would give me cookies or let me help her in the kitchen.

I was very close to my mother because I was always left behind with her. Karole was my father's constant companion since age five, and she never formed a close bond with our mother. Karole and my mother often did not see eye to eye, and Karole took my father's side in every disagreement.

My mother tried to protect me because of the way my father treated me. She continued to accuse Karole of being the only reason my father treated me the way he did. The anger my mother inflicted on my sister was a heavy load to carry. Karole should have hated me for the pain I caused her, but she never did. It was quite the opposite; Karole always looked out for me.

Oliver was a regular hunter and became friends with our father. He often conversed with Karole and me, and we enjoyed his company. We felt very comfortable when he was around. He was like the grandfather we never had.

Karole confided in Oliver one day about the many surnames we had used. She didn't realize she was doing anything wrong and didn't know that she had unwittingly alerted Oliver to something amiss in our family. This led Oliver to ask my father why he felt it necessary to change his family's identity so many times.

I never saw my father so angry with Karole. He screamed at the top of his lungs, telling her she had a big mouth and had ruined everything. He then took her out to the barn with the tractor belt in his hand. I heard the crack of the belt, but she did not cry out. When she returned to the house, she rushed into our bedroom, slammed the door shut, and refused to come out for dinner. I took a plate of food to her, but she told me to "go away."

My father spent the following week taking all twenty of our horses to auction and gave Gypsy and Moses to a neighbor.

Then he told us we were leaving... We had an hour to pack our suitcases... We were to take only our clothing and leave everything else behind.

That may have been the lowest point in my life.

After hours of driving, I overheard my father say to my mother, "Danielle will never be the same again." He couldn't have been more correct. Then, later added, "We are going back to the States."

At fifteen years old, I had figured out that we were running, but from what or whom, I didn't know.

An hour or so from the border crossing, my father instructed us...

"Karole and Danielle... Our last name is now Smith. Can you remember that?"

"Yes, Daddy," we replied in unison. We knew what was expected of us and didn't question our father's wisdom.

"And lose your way of talking so people will not be suspicious of where we come from," he added.

We had no trouble crossing the border into the United States. Karole and I smiled politely at the guard—we had gotten good at this game—and my father turned on his charm and lied through his teeth.

After driving for a few hours, Karole whispered, "I think we're going to Chicago!" We had seen pictures of Chicago in fashion magazines while standing in the grocery store checkout line. The ladies in Chicago wore short skirts and big floppy hats and carried huge purses. The streets were lined with fantastic stores, and we could only envision the experience of living in such a bustling city.

"We are not stopping in Chicago," my father overheard us talking and quickly ended our fantasy.

"Ma, where are we going this time?" Karole asked when we were in the ladies' room at a gas station and out of my father's earshot.

"You'll see when we get there." My mother answered, but I don't think she knew where we were going either.

My mother was a bundle of nerves—more nervous than usual.

"Ma," I asked. "What's wrong?"

"I accidentally forgot a suitcase… filled with important papers… behind the kitchen door," she stammered.

"That's okay, Ma," Karole consoled her. "We can get copies of what we need at our next house."

"No, we can't... You don't understand. That suitcase contained all our paperwork, receipts, and other identifying information."

Our mother handled all the bills and did the bookkeeping for the hunting camp or whatever business my father was involved in.

"Do NOT tell your father," she said as she left the restroom. "He'd kill me," she added under her breath.

"We won't, Ma!" Karole and I assured her.

We were traveling south, and the temperature was getting warmer each day. Occasionally, our mother let us hold the map. My sister and I scanned the roadside for street signs and pinpointed our location on the map. Our destination was always kept a secret, and I was beginning to think our parents wanted to prevent us from informing anyone we met along our journey about our final destination.

THIRTEEN

Goodlettsville

1973

WE NOT ONLY lied about our names; we lied about everything—our ages, the schools we had attended, and the cities in which we had lived. We even started speaking with a Southern accent. We could never be our true selves; lying became a significant part of our lives. It was all lies, lies, and more lies.

We stayed in a seedy motel for weeks. My parents left daily to search for jobs and a place to live. After a few weeks, they found a little brick house, and we moved in.

My first memory of the house was of my father cooking steaks on the grill. I made the mistake of saying I didn't want the one with the fat on it—fat upset my stomach. That evening at dinner, he instructed my mother and sister to cut the fat off their steaks and put it on my plate. I had to eat every bite.

One day, my father told my mother he wanted to look at some land for sale—I assumed he wanted to start another ranch. We climbed into our new Volkswagen Beetle and drove to the land. When we arrived, my father sent my mother and sister in one direction, while he and I went in the opposite direction.

We walked for some time. He told me what he was about to do would be our secret, and I could never tell anyone—not my mother, sister, or anyone else. I thought, "Wow! He is going to trust me with a secret... The kid he never wanted!" I was excited.

We ventured deep into the forest. The thick canopy of trees blocked most of the sunlight, but the ephemeral spring flowers bloomed wherever a ray of light broke through. I couldn't see my mother or sister anymore. It felt like my father and I were walking through a place no one had ever been. An eerie silence enveloped us; not a single bird could be heard.

I never felt that he loved me, but that day, he spoke to me in a way that made me feel loved. As we walked deeper into the forest, he told me that he was proud of the young woman I had become and that he had plans for my future. For the first time, I felt my father's love fill my heart.

He then said, "Lay down, Danielle." He took my hand and guided me to the forest floor. I thought he needed to rest for a while. He stood over me and unbuckled his belt. His breathing became rapid, and in what seemed like seconds, he was on top of me with his mouth on mine.

"Daddy!" I screamed as I turned my head to catch my breath. "Stop it, Daddy! Get off of me!" He forced his tongue into my mouth.

"Shut up, Danielle! You are a big girl now, and this is **what big girls do**!"

"You're hurting me!" I screamed again. I had never been so confused in my life. *Is this really what big girls do?*

With one hand, he pinned my hands above my head. His breath was hot and stank of cigarettes.

"Don't you know what you do to your Daddy?"

"What did I do? I'm sorry! I'm sorry, Daddy! Stop it! Please, you're hurting me!"

Did I do something wrong? Is this my punishment?

With his free hand, he pulled off my pink pedal pushers and panties and searched between my legs. He held my legs apart with his knees. I was a strong girl, but I was no match for him; he had me in a vice grip. He fumbled with his free hand, and after several attempts, he was inside of me.

The pain was searing, and I was sure that my insides were tearing. He thrust himself over and over for what seemed like an eternity until he let out a muffled scream.

He stood up, straightened himself out, and reached down to help me. He smoothed my hair and brushed the forest debris from my clothes.

"You are NOT to tell your mother what *we* just did. If you did, *you* would kill her. Then I would go to jail, and I would kill myself."

At fifteen, I did not have the first clue what sex was. I had seen dogs and horses do something similar to what had just happened to me, and it looked violent when they did it, too. My mother had once mentioned that she did *not* like her wifely duties —*was this what she meant by that?*

I felt dirty. The person who was supposed to protect me had just hurt me, and I could tell no one. We walked back to our car without speaking, and I felt the pain of what my father had done with every step I took.

We met up with my mother and sister, who were already standing next to the car. I forced a smile as we approached and held back my tears. I couldn't tell my mother; he had warned me what would happen if I did. Karole looked at me, and her mouth opened as if she wanted to say something, but instead, she opened the car door and got in.

"Danielle, you have leaves in your hair," my mother said as she picked them out.

"She fell," my father quickly added.

On the way home, we stopped at a grocery store. My father threw a handful of my favorite candy bars into the shopping cart.

My life was now defined as before and after. "Before" was when I was simply afraid of my father's temper and the sting of the tractor belt on my behind. The "after" world was frightening. Everything was different. The birds no longer sang, and a shower no longer made me feel clean. I found no joy in living. Food tasted bland, so why did I bother to eat? Every memory from my childhood was now divided into two very separate categories—the before... and the after.

Could I ever look at my father again? Could I ever converse with him? Could I be in a room alone with him? How would I function? Would my mother figure out what happened? Would she be angry with me? Would she blame me?

I moved through life robotically. I woke up early every morning and completed my chores without being asked. Whenever he entered a room, I left. If he spoke to me, I responded with as few words as possible. I didn't choose to act this way toward him. It was as if my soul was trying to protect me by keeping me out of his path.

The rewards began to arrive. Each time he returned from a business trip, he brought a gift. The first time, it was a new paisley dress; the second, a wristwatch; and the third, a fringed leather purse. Karole looked at me knowingly when I opened my gifts—she knew what I had done to earn them.

I feared my father before the incident, but after being raped, that fear intensified. I paced like an animal for days, asking myself a million times if this behavior between a father and daughter was normal. Was this what fathers did to teach their daughters to grow up? Was this what was expected of me? Was it what big girls did? Every hug or kiss filled me with dread, wondering what his touch would lead to.

I began dressing differently, opting for baggy pants and oversized sweatshirts to cover as much skin as possible. I walked with my head down and hunched my shoulders, concealing my figure.

When my mother went to the grocery store, he insisted she take Karole along. (My mother always followed his instructions.) He would insist that I accompany him on errands in town. He found clever ways to isolate me and raped me over and over again.

Sometimes, he chose Karole over me, leaving me behind. It didn't matter which of us he decided to take with him; I felt the same way. My stomach was tied in a permanent knot.

The price of land in Tennessee was much higher than in Athabaska, so he abandoned his dream of starting another ranch and gave up his profitable "Smiley-Face Button" business to avoid being traced.

He purchased a recipe for an eyeglass cleaner, and our family was focused on our next business venture. Mother cooked the potion on the stove and scooped it into three coffee pots. Karole and I filled little bottles, let them cool, and labeled them. He instructed Karole and me that we would be responsible for sales.

Our father visited malls and pharmacies to secure spots for us to sell the cleaner. My sister and I worked from 9 a.m. to 9 p.m., demonstrating and selling the cleaner. At first, he was pleased with our sales, but it was our fault if we had a bad day. He would shout at us and make us repeat our pitch over and over again until he was satisfied.

We traveled with him throughout the southern states to market the cleaner—our mother always remained behind. As my sister slept in the back seat, he would fondle me. I was always afraid she would wake up and catch him—I would have died of embarrassment. Yet, she never woke up, or maybe she did and ignored what was happening.

My father had an agreement with a chain of drugstores in New Orleans that allowed him to sell his eyeglass cleaner in front of their stores. We rented a motel for a few nights, so Karole and I could work at one of the stores to determine if the location would be profitable.

Early one morning, my father asked me to get a newspaper. When I returned to the hotel room, I was horrified when I opened the door... My father was in bed on top of my sister. I quickly closed the door, remaining on the outside. He thought I would be away longer, and he didn't properly lock the door.

I dropped the newspaper and started walking in the opposite direction, then broke into a run. How would I ever return to the room, and what would I say? After an hour, I knew I had to go back. The drugstore would open soon, and Karole and I had to go to work.

"There was a spider in your sister's bed, so she had to sleep in my bed," he said when I returned. It was a feeble explanation, even for him. I glanced at my sister to gauge her reaction. Her face showed no emotion. My heart sank, and I acted as if nothing out of the ordinary had happened.

After a month on the road, going from one drug store to the next, we finally returned home. It was then, in the privacy of our bedroom, that I found the courage to ask Karole the question that had been on my mind...

"How long has he been doing this to you?"

"Forever," she said calmly. Her reaction surprised me. I anticipated tears, but instead, she began brushing her hair in front of the mirror.

"I knew what he was going to do to you in Tennessee when we went to look at that land," she said matter-of-factly, "but I had no way of warning you. He always threatened to kill me if I told anyone." She applied lip gloss and puckered her lips as she gazed into the mirror.

"It was horrible, Karole! He warned me not to tell Ma. He said she would hate me if I did; then he would go to jail, and he would kill himself!" I said with terror in my voice.

"Would that be so bad?" my sister said flippantly as she twisted her thick dark hair into a knot.

"We can't tell Ma, Karole! She would cry forever."

Karole turned away from the mirror and locked her eyes on mine. "Maybe Ma knows what he's doing to us. Did you ever think of that?" Her eyes pierced me as if she wanted to drive her point deep into my soul.

"No! Ma doesn't know!" I protested.

"It's too late to tell her anyway. It's been going on for so long. Besides, I'm going to get out of here soon. I'm going to find a boyfriend and get the fuck away from him," she said while studying her reflection in the mirror. "I know what boys want, and I can give it to them." Karole was beautiful and aware that her attractiveness could be advantageous.

"That's a silly idea, Karole!" I half-laughed. "You have no time to meet a boy. We are always working!" Part of me wanted her to escape, but another part wanted her never to leave.

How long had he treated her like this, and did she consider it typical fatherly behavior? I resented him but didn't detect any hatred in Karole's tone. She didn't express her feelings towards him the way I expected. It seemed as if she neither loved nor hated him.

I felt trapped and resigned—there was no way out. I believed the cruel words my father spoke to me every day for as long as I could remember... "You're stupid, Danielle. You have no education, and no one will ever want you. You're a lazy, worthless human being."

I could never survive on my own.

Whenever my mother left for the grocery store or sewing lessons, my sister and I would plead with her to take us along. However, my father insisted that only one of us could accompany her, leaving the other behind. As hard as we tried to stay together, he dismissed one of us, and we understood what was happening in the other's absence.

He was controlling toward my mother. He asked her to make a nice meal every Sunday, but then, without fail, would yell about her cooking. He never gave her much money; if she spent what he gave her, she had to explain how and where.

In contrast, he bought her nice things and always remembered her birthday and their anniversary. He spoke highly of her to others and always said, "If someone doesn't like your mother, there is something wrong with them."

On one hand, he was kind and generous; on the other, he took everything away.

We sold eyeglass cleaners in stores, malls, and county fairs, and my father paid us each twenty dollars a week for our work.

My sister met Houston in New Orleans, and they started dating. Despite my father's disapproval, their relationship had value… Houston agreed to drive my sister and me from New Orleans to Alabama to sell the eyeglass cleaner at a drugstore. He appeared eager to remain in New Orleans while we traveled and was delighted when we came back with a pile of cash a week later.

In the hotel room that evening, Karole informed my father that she wasn't going home with us; she was moving in with Houston. My father became furious. He screamed into her face, telling her that Houston only wanted her for sex. But Karole stood firm. She had made up her mind. She packed her suitcase and left that night.

I then became the sole focus of my father's attention. The pressure soon became too much for me, so I packed a bag and hopped on a bus to be with my sister and her boyfriend. However, when I arrived, Karole told me she had been receiving threatening phone calls from my father and was afraid for her and Houston's safety. She insisted that I leave and sent me back home.

When I returned home the next day, the doors were locked. I knocked repeatedly and pleaded to be let back in, hitting the door until my fists were sore. I had nowhere else to go. At last, the door swung open.

"If you pull a stunt like this again, Danielle, I will never let you back in."

"I won't, Daddy. I promise."

Living on the streets seemed like my only other option, yet I didn't know how to make that happen. I was unaware of safe houses that could have provided shelter, and I didn't trust the police.

I knew nothing about survival outside my father's control, but I was determined to find a way out. I promised myself that the next time I left home, I would be prepared and never return, no matter what it took. However, I still needed to figure out what it would take to achieve my goal.

We left Goodlettsville and spent several months in Eufaula, Alabama, then several months in New Orleans, and on to Uriah, Alabama. Under my father's supervision, I sold eyeglass cleaners in each city for twelve hours every day, seven days a week.

Years passed, and I obediently followed my father's commands. When he abused me, I no longer fought him—to fight was futile. The more I fought, the more he threatened. Sometimes, it felt as if my mind left my body during the abuse, and I was in warm, loving arms that waited for me. It was the price I paid to survive. After all, I was a stupid, worthless human being, and nobody would ever want me.

FOURTEEN

Albuquerque

1978

MY FATHER HEARD good things about Albuquerque and saw an opportunity to expand the eyeglass cleaner business.

Albuquerque appeared to be a charming town, albeit a bit brown. Everything was new to me, and the locals were warm and welcoming.

Shortly after settling in, my mother was in a car accident that left her with internal injuries and a broken pelvis. I don't recall how long she was hospitalized, but it seemed like an eternity. I visited her daily until visiting hours were over, and the nurses almost had to throw me out. I didn't want to leave... I knew who and what I was going home to and what awaited me.

I pleaded with the doctors to allow her to come home, promising to take care of her. Eventually, they agreed to discharge her earlier than usual if I pledged to clean and dress her surgical wound every day.

I helped her to the bathroom, assisted her in the shower, and supported her in regaining her walking ability. I also prepared meals and kept the house clean. It made my heart happy to repay her for all she had done for me, and I was glad to have her back in the house… for more than one reason.

At twenty years old, I needed to gain skills and self-confidence. I had been sheltered from the world, constantly moving, and never stayed in one place long enough to form meaningful connections with anyone outside the family. My sister and I toiled like slaves trapped by a spell and were conditioned to obey our father's every command. We never dared to question him. Voicing a disagreement would provoke his temper, something we were all too familiar with, and we did anything to avoid it.

Why didn't I just escape? Why didn't I tell him to leave, report him to the police, and never look back? I didn't realize I had choices or that I could make decisions for myself.

We spent our lives running, hiding, and changing our identities. I shared my father's fear of the police, even though there was no logic behind it. For most of my childhood, my sister and I were kept hidden and confined. We were raised in a physical and mental prison, and we did not develop the ability to think independently.

After leaving Manotick, we never contacted relatives from my mother's or father's side again. I had no aunts, uncles, or grandparents to confide in. I was never taken to a doctor, so confiding in a trusted adult didn't seem like an option. From my perspective, the world was filled with strangers. I had been taught not to trust anyone outside our nuclear family.

We lived in cars, motels, mobile homes, apartments, and houses. Even when we had land to roam, my sister and I were no better off than animals in a cage.

Ironically, I only felt free when we left for another part of the country. I was free to look out the car window and wonder about the world. What activities were taking place in other houses? What were the children learning in the schools? Why was smoke billowing from the factories? What were they making inside the buildings?

I noticed parents walking with their children on the sidewalks. Did the fathers also control every aspect of their lives? Did the wives have to account for every penny they spent? And did the other fathers do to their daughters what my father did to me?

My chronological age didn't reflect my level of maturity. I was skilled at handling hay bales, caring for horses, and persuading people to buy my products, but I struggled with interpersonal relationships outside my family circle.

The only area I felt confident in was my physical ability to outwork anyone my age. Engaging in meaningful discussions on topics that didn't revolve around physical labor or eyeglass cleaners was challenging. I found it difficult to maintain eye contact and express myself when strangers asked personal questions, as my parents often spoke on my behalf.

After two years, Karole's relationship with Houston ended, and she found herself back on our doorstep, begging to be let back in. She had put on a considerable amount of weight and was almost unrecognizable. When she started dating Houston, she could have been a fashion model.

"What happened to you!" Father yelled at her. "You're fat!"

Karole seemed to expect a certain amount of insults from our father as her punishment for leaving home. She rarely called during her two-year absence, and I missed her terribly.

"Our last name is now Watson." Father barked at Karole. "And my first name is Raymond. What is my name?"

"Your name is Raymond Watson," she replied flatly, accepting the information as a re-admission into the family.

My mother didn't comment on Karole's weight gain. The next day, she served Swiss steak with no gravy and string beans for dinner, replaced the sugar bowl with Equal, and poured Karole a glass of Tab instead of milk.

My sister and I were back to selling eyeglass cleaners in the mall. People seemed to sense the desperation in our voices as we hawked our product; we made more sales than the other kiosks. We would face our father's anger if we didn't sell enough. I detested everything about sales and knew that when I was on my own, I would never work in sales again.

Karole and me

We maintained a reserved and professional tone in our interactions with our customers… until Karole met Phil in front of Montgomery Ward.

Karole wanted to leave home again, so initially, I thought she was using Phil as a way out. However, I could see her genuine feelings for him after a few weeks.

My father was upset that Karole was in another relationship, which led to daily arguments.

"Phil doesn't love you. He's just using you for sex! That's what boys his age do!" he screamed at Karole. "You are *not* to see him again!"

"I love him, Daddy, and nothing you do will change that!" Karole stated boldly.

He slapped her face; she had dared to defy him. Her head jerked from the blow. She covered her face to lessen the sting but showed no fear.

My father was frantic. Karole would never be his again. He had worked all his life to make Karole strong, and now he faced the harsh reality of who he had created.

He was desperate to break up Karole and Phil, but he had signed a contract with the mall to sell at the kiosk, and Karole and I were earning enough money to cover the rent. Karole would meet with Phil at the mall, and my father could not stop it. So, instead, he stipulated that Karole and Phil had to take me on every one of their dates to serve as a chaperone.

Karole and Phil eloped to Las Vegas. On one hand, I was thrilled for her. Their courtship was quick, but they seemed perfect for each other. Phil worshiped the ground she walked on. Karole appeared genuinely happy, perhaps for the first time. On the other hand, I was devastated by her departure and was again left to deal with my father solo.

When Karole and Phil returned to Albuquerque, Karole got a job at a vision center in the mall, which was just a short distance from where I sold eyeglass cleaners. We talked every time she had a break and discussed everything from her marriage to my life. We had no secrets between us. Nobody else could understand what our lives had been like except for the two of us.

Every morning at nine, my father would drive me to the mall and pick me up twelve hours later when it closed. He wouldn't allow me to get a driver's license and controlled every aspect of my life. On the way home from the mall, he would ask me if I had my period. I always said yes, but he soon caught on to my deception. He would then park the car in a remote area and have his way with me.

I learned to dissociate; my mind shifted to another realm during the abuse. It was as if the events unfolded before me like a movie… or were happening to another person. At times, it felt like my spirit hovered above the trees, wrapped in the embrace of a caring presence that assured me everything would be all right.

As a child, my mother instilled in me a sense of spirituality. Even though we only attended church a handful of times, I still felt close to God. After the initial attack, I knelt and pleaded with God to protect me from my father's harm, but he didn't stop, and my prayers went unanswered.

I became desensitized to my father's voice, breath, touch, and presence. Despite being in his early sixties, he was a strong man. He applied every wrestling hold he had learned as a professional wrestler to overpower me. As hard as I fought, I was never strong enough, and eventually, I became exhausted.

Sometimes, when my mother looked at me, I saw sadness in her eyes, almost as if she felt sorry for me. She stayed busy with household chores most of the time, as she believed a good wife should.

I've thought about telling my mother about the abuse multiple times, but I remained keenly aware of the consequences, as he constantly reminded me of what they were…

The knowledge that her daughter had "encouraged him" would kill my mother… She would hate me after finding out… He would be arrested and thrown in prison… And the prisoners would kill him… Or he would kill himself.

I held the sole responsibility of keeping the family intact. I didn't care about my father's fate; he deserved whatever happened to him. But I would rather harm myself than ever harm my mother.

FIFTEEN

Albuquerque

1982

Danielle, Theresa, and Karole, January 1982

WE HAD SEVERED ties with relatives on my mother's side long ago. However, my father occasionally contacted one of his relatives when he found their name in the phone book.

I met my cousin Jimmy (the son of my father's sister) for the first time when he visited us in Albuquerque. It was hard to believe that he was related to my father. My father was stocky and dark, while Jimmy was tall, light-complected, and willowy.

I had a fantastic time with Jimmy. It was the first time I had fun with someone my age. Jimmy would meet me after I finished working, and we would go to a local bar to play pool. I was a beginner at the game but became adept and playfully competitive by the third night, thanks to Jimmy's instruction.

Jimmy bought me my first beer, and I loved how I felt when I drank it. Besides making me want to laugh, having a beer made me feel as if I were one of them. It made me feel like I "fit in" with everyone else at the tavern. With a beer in one hand and a cue stick in the other, I was no different from anyone else.

In the middle of a game, Jimmy set down his cue stick and turned to me with a serious expression.

"Danielle, I think you should know something…"

"What is it?" The look on his face scared me.

"Many years ago, the police came to our house. They asked my mother questions about your father. They wanted to know where he was. Of course, she had no clue where he was and had no information to provide them."

"What reason did the police give for interrogating her?"

"They didn't tell her why he was wanted, but they looked plenty pissed. They told my mother to contact them immediately if she heard from him."

I took aim at the cue ball, snapped the eight ball into the corner pocket, and then turned to face Jimmy. He was staring at me, awaiting my reaction.

"You know… We always suspected your father was running from the law. That must have been hard on you as a kid."

"I eventually figured out that we were running, but from what always remained a mystery."

"That must have been very confusing for you," he added.

"Confusing is an understatement."

"You must have attended many different schools... Adjusting can be difficult. Kids can be cruel, and curricula can vary from school to school," he said sympathetically.

"You have no idea," I said as I racked the balls for the next game. I wanted to confess to him that I had no formal education, but I held my tongue. Jimmy had the kindest eyes, and I felt I could trust him. However, the information could spread to his parents, and my father would have my head on a platter if he found out I was giving away family secrets.

While Jimmy stayed at our house, my father and I arrived home one evening after a demanding workday. I had barely made any sales, and my father began to yell at me…

"You are useless, Danielle! Did you use the pitch I told you to say? No! I'm sure you didn't because you're a stupid, stupid girl!"

I was accustomed to his treatment of me, and it didn't shock me. This was routinely how I was scolded for not bringing home enough money. At that moment, Jimmy walked out of the kitchen, holding a plate with a sandwich. His jaw dropped; he had heard my father berate me.

"And you are a bad influence on her!" My father turned his focus to Jimmy. "You are done here. You have overstayed your welcome!"

Jimmy went to his room, packed his suitcase, and left the house within minutes. I wanted to crawl under my bed and never come out.

After Jimmy left, I tossed and turned, trying to fall asleep, but a voice in my head nagged at me. I could not stop seeing the look on Jimmy's face when my father turned on him; it was seared into my brain. Of course, I didn't react to my father, but when I saw Jimmy's face turn white, it awakened something in me. My father's rage was part of my everyday life, but seeing it through Jimmy's eyes made me realize it was anything but ordinary.

My bedroom window was the only window in the house on which my father had not installed an alarm. As he got older, his paranoia seemed to worsen. I didn't know who he thought would try to enter our house while we slept, but he believed someone would.

As I lay in my bed, I thought of putting a stick in the window, but he would kill me if I did. He was furious after Jimmy left, and I knew he wanted to punish me. He could climb through the window at any moment, cover my mouth, and whisper how worthless I was as he forced himself on me.

My eyes started to close due to sheer exhaustion, but the moment they did, I was startled awake, convinced the window had begun to slide open.

I rose from bed, pondering how long I would continue to live in fear of my father. At twenty-three, I hadn't progressed beyond fifteen, the year the sexual abuse began.

It was now or never.

It was cold outside, and I knew I might have to sleep on the street. I put on three sweatshirts and two pairs of pants, then put on my boots and packed my shoes in a paper bag. Next, I opened my dresser drawers and took out the items that meant the most to me: a hairbrush, my only tube of lipstick, hand lotion, and a fancy bar of soap I had received at Christmas and hadn't used yet. I couldn't think straight; terror blocked rational thinking. What if he opened my bedroom door? How would I explain that I am packing?

I suddenly remembered my blue ribbon. I had hidden it under the mattress. I knelt, lifted the mattress with one hand, and searched with the other. "Where is it?" I whispered into the dark room. If I could have turned on the light, that would have helped, but he'd see the light coming from under my door, and out of curiosity, he'd open it. My fingers searched until I found it, and I tucked it into the paper bag.

I stuffed clothes into the bag until I heard the seams starting to give. I put on a jacket, gloves, and a stocking cap. I dumped a jar of money I had saved into my jacket pocket.

My father's plan to not install an alarm on my window backfired on him that night as I quietly slid the window open and climbed out. The bitterly cold air took my breath away, but I welcomed it; it helped me think clearly. I walked backward a few steps, then stood still, staring back at the house. I clutched the grocery bag. I had $100 in my pocket. I had no job. I had no car.

"What am I doing?" I whispered into the air. "He'll find me!"

My feet refused to move. The world was a scary place, but so was my home. I could call Karole, but there was no guarantee she would let me stay with her. She had sent me home in the past because she feared our father's wrath. That scenario would likely repeat itself. Father would call her in the morning and demand she send me back. A part of me wanted to slide the window open and crawl back in. After all, I was damaged goods. And who would ever want me?

A payphone outside of Pizza Hut became my goal. I turned and began to run. Minutes into my escape, a helicopter flew overhead. *Are they looking for me? Did Daddy discover I was gone and call the police? Did he see my footprints in the snow?* I took cover under an oak tree in someone's front yard, waiting until the helicopter was gone, and then took off again. I laughed as I ran, realizing that my level of paranoia was ridiculous.

I struggled with the coins in my pocket until I found a dime. My cold hands trembled as I tried to insert the coin into the slot. I missed, and the dime fell to the floor. I searched the filthy floor until I found it.

I dialed my sister, hoping that I could speak coherently through my frozen lips when she answered —*if* she answered. Her phone began to ring. It was 2 a.m., and I knew she would be fast asleep. She had to get up early for work in the morning.

Please, please answer...

"Hello?" Karole replied, her voice thick with sleep.

"Karole! Thank God you answered!"

"Danielle? Why are you calling me at this hour?"

"I ran away! Don't tell me to go home this time, Karole! I can't live with him anymore and have nowhere to go!"

"Where are you?"

"I'm right outside of the Pizza Hut. Do you know where that is?"

"I do. Hold on…" She put her hand over the phone, and I heard her muffled voice speaking to Phil. "Danielle? We're coming. Stay there." *Click.*

The town was eerily quiet. Neon signs lit up the street outside each establishment. I ducked into the entryway to the Pizza Hut and didn't move a muscle. I set down my grocery bag. Somewhere along the way, the bag had torn further, and one shoe and some clothing items were missing. My blue ribbon was also gone. I had left a trail of breadcrumbs behind.

I whispered, "Oh, my God," a hundred times. It was the only way I could think of to pray. I hoped that God heard me and understood that I needed His help. I focused on the sound of my breath and tried to calm myself.

Nearly an hour later, Karole and Phil pulled up alongside the curb in their rusty Ford Pinto.

"Danielle!" Karole called out from the car window. I emerged from the shadow of my hiding place as she opened the door and exited the car. Her eyes were fixed on my torn grocery bag. She looked down the street.

"Wait a minute…" She walked down the street to collect some items that had fallen out of my bag.

"Danielle, is this your shoe? And are these your shirts?"

"They are!" I was grateful for her ability to think clearly in a stressful situation. I was far too fearful to look back.

When Karole and I got into the car, Phil turned around and looked at me. "Are you okay? You look cold."

"I'm fine," I lied. I couldn't feel my fingers or toes.

"Karole sent you back home the last time you ran away, but she was living with Houston then. Things are different now, and I'm not afraid of your father."

"You don't know him, Phil! He has a horrible temper, and he's powerful! He's got guns!"

"I have a gun, too. He's an old man. He doesn't scare me." Phil spoke with confidence.

"No matter how upset our father gets, Phil and I will stand behind you this time. You can stay with us as long as necessary," Karole reassured me. Those were the most beautiful words I could have heard at that moment.

When my father realized I was missing the following morning, he immediately called Karole.

"I have no idea where Danielle is," she sounded convincing. She had learned to lie from the best. As she spoke, I recalled her being swung by her ponytail. She showed no fear then and showed no fear now.

After she hung up the phone, she turned to me... "Danielle, was he still…"

"He slowed down the past few years," I answered quickly, not wanting to go into detail. I could happily live in denial and never discuss what my father did to me for the rest of my life.

"He's in his sixties, for God's sake. I thought he'd stopped that nonsense a long time ago." Her chin quivered as she realized that moving forward with her life meant leaving me behind.

"Karole, it's not your fault. You had to leave. I get that."

After Karole left for work, I took a cereal box from the cabinet and sat at the kitchen table. I was hungry but couldn't eat, so I thought about the day ahead…

Karole told my father I wasn't with her, but did he suspect she was lying? Would he come to look for me? What if I walked down the sidewalk, and he pulled his car up next to me… Would I get in? Was this what it was like to be a slave who escaped her master? Freedom was something I had dreamed of. But I felt anything but free.

I walked the sidewalks of the downtown area, entering every establishment with a "help wanted" sign in the window. I filled out several job applications and lied about graduating from high school. I wasn't sure if they would check my background, and I felt anxious for days, worrying they would find out I was a fraud. After a while, lying on the applications became second nature. I started to wonder if I was doing the right thing or if I would go to hell for deceiving the business owners.

In a few weeks, I was hired as a snack bar attendant at a bowling alley. I enjoyed the sound of bowling balls hitting the pins and the cheers when the bowlers made strikes. I was grateful that my mother had taught me how to count money and give change when I was twelve. I was better at it than most of my coworkers with high school diplomas.

When I received my first paycheck, I was amazed that I could earn over twenty dollars a week without getting yelled at. It was an incredible feeling.

Within weeks, I was offered the manager position at the bowling alley with a significant raise. The owner was impressed by my work ethic and told me that I was doing the work of three people.

I accepted the promotion, but my secret loomed... With no education, how would I manage the books?

My brother-in-law volunteered to teach me basic math. We spent hours at the kitchen table every evening after dinner while he patiently explained addition, subtraction, multiplication, and division to me. I bought multiplication flashcards and studied them until I memorized them. I was determined to succeed.

While focusing on my job, I didn't have time to dwell on my past. Hard work was my escape. It was only when I finished work for the day that thoughts of my father flooded back. Part of me felt he still had control over me and could return to take over at any moment. I couldn't shake the fear and lived with the uncertainty of not knowing what would happen next.

Life without my mother felt empty, but my father guarded her, his precious commodity, to regain control over me. The only way to see her was to cross the imaginary bridge he governed, which kept us apart. We both needed his permission to cross it.

Several months after I left home, my father entered the bowling alley and found me working at my desk.

"Is there any coffee in this place?" he asked casually as if no time or sin had passed between us.

His white polo shirt was tucked into his jeans, and his belt strained to keep his pants up. His hair and mustache had gotten whiter, and his face had wrinkled.

"What are you doing here, Daddy?" I was stunned; he was the last person I expected to see that day.

"Can't a father come to see his daughter?" he said in a friendly manner, masking the underlying irritation only recognizable to those who knew him well.

My first instinct was to close the door in his face. I was still a puppet controlled by his tightly gripped strings, manipulated at will. He would still be abusing me if I hadn't found the courage to leave.

I stood straight and tall in my navy blue suit and black pumps and agreed to a coffee. As we walked toward the snack bar, he looked like a little old man I could quickly shove to the side if I chose to. I could effortlessly lean toward his bloated face and give him a piece of my mind. Maybe it was the self-confidence I gained from my position as a manager, but for the first time in my life, he posed no threat to me. *What had been so scary about him?* He smiled and winked at the waitress behind the snack counter as we sat.

"Danielle, you look good," he said as he studied my appearance. "I like your hair that length."

"Thank you," I answered meekly as I felt myself pulled back in time.

"Danielle, your mother misses you. It's time for you to come home."

"I miss Ma, too. Why hasn't she called me back?"

"She's angry that you left, Danielle." There it was… the ammunition he had been waiting to use against me.

When I ran away from home, I didn't consider what it would do to my relationship with my mother. I never thought that by leaving, our relationship would abruptly come to a halt.

I had called my mother every week since I left—she never answered. The last time I called, I left a message asking her to come to the bowling alley to meet me for lunch. Of course, she did not return my call, but my father must have intercepted the message and tracked me down.

"Can you tell Ma to call me?" I pleaded, even though I already knew his answer. The last time I talked to my mother was the evening before I left home.

"She won't call you," he curtly answered. He was using my relationship with my mother as leverage. He would *never* allow her to call or visit me unless we struck a bargain he could benefit from.

"I can't come home. I have a good job. I'll get an apartment as soon as I save up enough money. It's time for me to live on my own." I amazed myself—I stood up to him.

He looked around the bowling alley as if sizing up the responsibility I had taken on.

"So, you're the manager here?" he asked.

"Yes, and I make ten dollars an hour." I wanted him to calculate just how well I was doing. My salary was significantly higher than the twenty dollars a week he had paid me, not to mention the tirades I endured if I didn't meet the impossible quotas he set.

I suspected he was impressed with what I had accomplished. I had a decent job despite being conditioned to feel worthless every single day of my life.

"How is Karole?" he asked, fishing for confirmation of where I was living.

"She's fine. She has a good job, and Phil is a good husband."

I stopped myself from saying more. Karole did not want him to know where she lived or where she worked.

My sister told me she had read a book about Stockholm syndrome... "Sometimes," she said, "people who are held captive rationalize physical and emotional abuse. They believe their captor is correct and that they, the captives, deserve the abuse they receive."

Karole thought that we had developed a negative attitude on behalf of our father toward anyone who threatened our way of life. Therefore, we never felt secure seeking help from the authorities.

Other people who had experienced Stockholm syndrome probably had a normal life to return to once they realized what had happened to them. "Normal" was as unfamiliar to me as a trip to another planet. My entire life, I had been living in Stockholm syndrome; I had no idea what normal was and didn't know how to find it. However, I would never have discovered a normal life if I had gone home to live with him again. I had tasted freedom, and there was no going back.

He now treated me with respect, the way I always wanted him to, and I interpreted his new attitude toward me as his way of apologizing. He never mentioned what he did to me, although sometimes I thought I saw sadness in his eyes.

Part of me loathed him for his actions, while another part didn't. I convinced myself he regretted the abuse he inflicted. In his distorted mindset, he believed he was teaching me to be a woman or disciplining me because he thought I was a stupid, lazy, useless human being. The other option was to believe he was evil and perverted. He once told me that my mother denied him his rightful marital relations. I thought of many reasons for his actions, but they all came to the same conclusion: His soul was broken.

He alone had the power to help me mend my relationship with my mother, so I agreed to have coffee with him regularly. For the first time, I felt empowered and secure. I had friends, and I was on top of the world. Most importantly, I felt superior to him.

"Are you getting an apartment soon and leaving your sister's place? I'm sure Karole and Phil would like to have their apartment to themselves."

I knew what he was doing. He wanted me to admit I was living with Karole. "Maybe I'll visit you and bring your mother with me," he added slyly.

It was a trick, and I caught on immediately. He dangled a reunion with my mother before me… if I cooperated.

I took a deep breath and found my courage.

"I want to see Ma," I stated firmly, giving him no room to argue my point.

I had never spoken to him in that tone—he was stunned. He stared at me, searching for the words to answer. I could almost hear his gears turning as he wondered if I now possessed the strength he always wanted me to have. Was I finally strong enough to confess everything he did to my mother?

"Call her tonight," he finally answered. "I'll see that she answers."

At eight o'clock that evening, I dialed…

"Hello, Ma?" I choked out.

"Hello, Danielle," she said sadly.

Was the sadness in her voice because she feared him? She missed me? Or was she living with the knowledge of what he did to her daughters? I quickly snapped myself out of that thought process. She could not possibly have known. How could she have? Karole and I never said a word.

Our conversation consisted of small talk. My father stood nearby and chimed in to let me know she wasn't alone.

The following day, my father brought my mother to the bowling alley. I was so happy to see her! I walked them to the snack bar and ordered nachos and Cokes for lunch.

The sound of bowling pins cracking in the background and cheers from the bowlers saved us from having to converse. Finally, my mother inquired about my job. How did I like it? Was the boss nice to me? Did I actually have to hire and fire people? My father never left us alone for a minute, and when my break was over, my mother hugged me goodbye, which was unusual since she wasn't typically demonstrative with affection.

After they left, I couldn't help but wonder: What were his visits to the bowling alley about? Was he proud of me, or was I just a curiosity to him? Was he amazed at what I had accomplished despite his lifelong put-downs? Or was it his last-ditch effort to intimidate, manipulate, and show me he still had control over me?

I felt the need to be the best at work, at home, and even during fun activities. I was on a mission to prove myself to the detriment of anyone unfortunate enough to be in my way.

I chased success, believing it would finally relieve the persistent knot in my stomach. The knot was present when I went to bed at night and returned with force when I woke up. In my drive to seek validation, I hurt people who stood in my way—I equated success with love.

SIXTEEN

Albuquerque

1984

WHEN THE APARTMENT above the bowling alley became available, and the owner offered it to me, I jumped at the opportunity and moved in the following day. It was my first time living alone, and I was skeptical. Karole and her husband had been gracious hosts for over a year but needed their space.

I wasn't sure what to do with my newfound freedom, so I spent evenings browsing the local stores to buy decorative items. I purchased blue-striped towels for the bathroom and yellow dish towels for the kitchen. I found a tall, blue decorative vase for my kitchen table and vowed to keep it filled with flowers. I also found a floral bedspread with matching pillows for my bed. As I made the apartment my own, I began to enjoy living alone, and every time I walked into it, I felt it welcomed me with a warm hug.

Every night before bed, I would check all the window locks and wedge a chair in front of the door.

Below my apartment, the sounds from the bowling alley continued late into the night, and I became accustomed to them. However, at the same time, the noise of the pins falling could easily drown out the sound of a window breaking or a door being forced open.

I was proud of my accomplishments since I left home. Customers often praised my strong work ethic and remarked that they had never seen someone my age work so hard.

I organized bowling leagues, oversaw the snack bar and food ordering, managed employee turnover, supervised cleaning crews, hired workers to repair equipment, and handled rowdy, drunken customers. I tackled each problem as if I were born to do the work.

A member of the Thursday evening league, Jess, started showing interest in me. I was unsure how to handle his flirting, and I attributed his attention to the fact that he was drinking too much beer.

"Hey, Danielle!" he called out when I passed by. "When are ya gonna let me take ya on a date?" His buddies began to tease and elbow him.

"Hey, old man," one of his friends chimed in. "She's a little young for you, don't you think?!"

I kept my head down and kept walking. As I prepared to leave my office one evening, Jess appeared in the doorway.

"Hey, Danielle!"

"Hi," I looked up briefly and businesslike. I did not want to encourage him.

"So, what are ya doing this weekend?"

"I'm working," I said curtly as I shuffled papers on my desk, hoping he would get the hint and go away.

"How 'bout we go to a movie on Saturday after ya get off work?"

My heart was pounding. Was I being ridiculous? I had known Jess since I worked at the snack bar. He had a laid-back personality, and everyone loved him. In no way did he pose a threat. He was a paying customer, but I knew what men wanted. I maintained my professionalism and continued working.

"I'm swamped now, Jess…"

"Cheech and Chong is playing at the cinema. I think ya could use a good laugh, Danielle. Do ya wanna go?"

I had made a life for myself, but my confidence disappeared when an older man spoke to me—I felt fifteen years old again.

"I'll be done with work at seven on Saturday," I answered, still shuffling papers.

"Good! I'll pick ya up here. You know, we have a lot in common… I manage the Ranchero Bowl in Rio Rancho. We'll have lots to talk about." Jess smiled.

"If you work at Ranchero Bowl, why do you belong to a league here?"

"Cause all my friends are here."

"Oh, I see."

I wanted to tell him he was too old for me, but I knew I'd hurt his feelings if I did. Besides, Karole had been encouraging me to have some fun. Hanging out with Jess might be enjoyable.

Jess talked about himself as we sat across from one another in the booth. He spoke fast and probably told me more than he should have on our first date. I thought he seemed nervous.

"Me and my ex-wife share custody of our kids, but the bitch hardly lets them visit me! She won't let me step foot in her house, formerly *my* house! I have a decent apartment now, so there is no reason in hell they can't spend more time with me."

"Tell me more about your job?" I redirected the conversation.

"Me and you have identical jobs. The pay is decent, but I don't have two nickels to rub together after paying child support and my bills."

Suddenly, I found myself struggling to swallow my hamburger. Perhaps he couldn't even afford to take me to a fast-food restaurant. He supported an ex-wife and two children and seemed to have difficulty affording much else.

"It's good that you can afford the bowling league, a few beers, and cigarettes," I said, trying to lighten the mood. I felt sorry for him.

"Are ya saying I'm wasting my money on having a little fun?" My remark annoyed him; he believed I was judging him.

"No, that's not what I meant at all!" I was horrified. I did not intend to insult him, and he quickly became defensive.

Since Jess had paid for our dinner, I offered to pay for the movie, but he flatly refused my offer.

"Call me old-fashioned, but a man should treat a woman respectfully when courtin' her."

I was shocked. Being treated with respect was nice. But was he courting me?

After the movie, he held my hand as we walked to his car.

"Do ya have that big apartment above the bowling alley all to yourself, Danielle?"

"I do, although I'm not sure I like living alone."

"You're grown up in so many ways, Danielle, but you're still a little girl on the inside, ain't ya?"

"What do you mean?" I was perplexed. I managed the bowling alley, and people looked up to me and respected me.

"I don't know, it's just something about ya. I guess it's in your eyes… You've got this wide-eyed look… like you're scared of what's around the corner."

"I'm not afraid of anything!" I said boldly. "I'm certainly not afraid of you," I added with a laugh. "Do you want a tour of my apartment?"

"I'd love that," he said with a grin.

I didn't see any harm in showing him my apartment. I was proud of it. Besides, I didn't particularly appreciate walking into the apartment alone in the middle of the night—it didn't feel safe. I turned the key, and we stepped inside.

"Wow! This *is* nice!" His eyes slowly took in every detail. "Ya don't have to pay any rent for this place?"

"No… It's one of the perks of the job."

"Are ya sure you didn't sleep with the owner?"

"No!" I didn't appreciate his humor.

"Sorry, that wasn't funny. You're a good girl, ain't ya?"

He began to walk from room to room and poked his head inside each one.

"Ya have two bedrooms! And two bathrooms!"

"I do. This place is too big for just one person. I'm thinking of getting a roommate."

"I'll be your roommate!" he enthusiastically offered.

"My sister is thinking of moving in," I quickly lied to end anything he was conjuring up.

"I'm just teasing ya. I have a decent apartment, and it's close to my kids and work."

I excused myself and went into the bathroom to splash cold water on my face. When I came out, I saw Jess closing my top dresser drawer.

"What are you looking for?" I said cautiously. I didn't want him to think I didn't trust him.

"Nothin'! I'm just checking out the quality of your furniture."

I was ready to end the date, so I led him to the door and explained that I had to get up early for work.

"Ya have to work on Sunday?!" he asked. "I never go to work on Sunday. Ya have to take some time off, girl."

"Well, families love to bowl on Sunday after church, and it just makes my life easier on Monday if I go in for a few hours on Sunday."

"Do you wanna do something tomorrow afternoon?" he quickly asked.

"What do you have in mind?"

"We can go for a drive. Maybe we can go on a picnic?" he asked with a boyish grin.

"I guess I could do that."

"Good! I'll bring a blanket and a bottle of wine."

He leaned in and quickly kissed my lips. I jerked my head back.

"Oh, I'm sorry… I thought it would be okay…"

"Goodnight, Jess," I said politely. I felt no attraction to him. *Why did I agree to go out with him again?*

Jess arrived early for our date the next day and followed me around the bowling alley, talking incessantly. I had at least an hour left to work, so I asked him if he wanted to pack our lunch. "I have a loaf of bread on the counter and some bologna in the refrigerator." He eagerly agreed, so I gave him the key to my apartment.

We drove the short distance to Hidden Park. I spread the blanket in the shade of a large oak tree, and then he offered his hand to help me sit down.

"Wow, you're such a gentleman!" His manners were old-fashioned but better than those of the immature men I had dated. He had even insisted on opening the car door for me.

"Of course! My mama raised me right!"

That day, I learned a lot about him. He had been divorced for two years; his daughter, Sharlee, was fourteen, and his son, Lance, was twelve. He seemed to lack ambition to improve his financial situation; he was satisfied managing the bowling alley and had no intention of pursuing anything further.

"So… A cute girl like you… You've probably had a lot of boyfriends, Danielle."

Due to the physical demands of my job, I didn't have any extra weight on my body. Additionally, I didn't have time to visit the hairdresser, so my hair was thick and long. Coincidentally, I was in the best shape of my life. I often received approving looks from male bowlers and heard catcalls when walking down the street, but I paid them no attention. With nothing else happening in my life besides work, time spent with Jess felt harmless.

I had been on my share of dates, and two of the relationships had become serious: Mark. After dating for several months, we moved in together. After work,

I cooked dinner and did my best to be the perfect "wife."

Intimacy with Mark was awkward and felt more like a chore, especially since we were young and unmarried, and I had a fear of getting pregnant. The Catholic part of me encouraged him to marry me, but he refused. After a few months of living together, we decided to go our separate ways.

Then there was Kelly. He made me feel something I had never felt: an electricity I had never experienced. However, Kelly was involved with drugs, and I found it necessary to end our relationship. The chemistry between us was exciting, but it wasn't enough.

"Do you always date younger women?" I was curious.

"You're the first woman I've dated since my divorce," he said thoughtfully.

I didn't believe him, but his expression remained solemn.

"Do you mean to tell me you haven't dated one woman since your divorce?"

"Well, I've slept with women if that's what you're gettin' at. But none of them meant a hill of beans to me. They were just for sex. You're the first woman to catch my eye in a long time."

His words made my head swim. Jess was the first mature man I had dated. In Mark's eyes, I felt desperate to be wanted. In Kelly's eyes, I felt intense sexual attraction. But in Jess's eyes, I felt respected and admired.

"So… did ya grow up here in Albuquerque?" he inquired.

"I've only lived here for six years."

"Where did ya grow up then?"

I had to stifle a laugh. *Where did I grow up?* I had to pause to gather my thoughts.

"I don't remember all the places I've lived, but I was born in Virginia. Then, I moved to Quebec City, followed by Vermont and Utah. After that, I lived in Manotick, Calgary, Ottawa, Vancouver, Coquitlam, Vancouver Island, Surrey, Athabasca, Goodlettsville, and finally Albuquerque." I took an exaggerated deep breath and then laughed to make my situation seem typical. "I'm sure I missed a dozen locations, and I do *not* guarantee the order… My childhood is a blur."

Jess stared at me; he was speechless.

"Where'd ya go to school?"

"I can't recall the names of the schools."

"Did ya go to college?"

"No!"

"Well, ya look like ya went to college." I was thrilled to hear him say those words. Whatever I was doing to fool the people was working. "What was going on in your life that caused your family to move so much?" he asked.

"I have no idea. I speculated over the years, but I've never gotten to the root of the problem. It always felt as if my father was running from something or someone. He was paranoid. Every time we moved, he changed our last name," I said again with a nervous laugh.

"That's *not* normal, Danielle," he said disapprovingly.

"I know that now, but I didn't as a kid."

"Did ya ever ask your parents why they moved so goddamn much?"

"No."

"Why the hell not?" He raised his eyebrows.

"I didn't question their decisions," I answered.

"What would happen if you did?"

"My father had a temper. I don't want to talk about him." I had already admitted far too much.

"Then is your last name really Watson?" Jess asked, curious.

"No. Watson is our most recent last name. I honestly can't tell you my legal surname… I've never been told. My parents were likely already on the run when I was born."

I didn't know why I was telling Jess so much. It wasn't like me to divulge my family's secrets. The words had poured out without hesitation.

I opened the paper bag and laid out the sandwiches and apples. Jess brought a bottle of red wine, two glasses, and a chocolate bar.

"Ouch!" I cried out. I had bit down too hard on my apple.

"What happened?" he asked.

"I have a toothache. I have a dental appointment next week, " I explained.

"Hey, tell your dentist to pull *all* your teeth! I've heard a girlfriend with no teeth is a good thing!" He laughed. I chose to ignore the innuendo—I didn't appreciate sexual jokes.

Once we finished lunch, we reclined on the blanket. I felt a sense of calm with Jess beside me, which caught me off guard; perhaps it was the wine.

I turned to my side to study him. His tightly curled, salt-and-pepper hair was short, contrasting with his long sideburns. He had trimmed his mustache that morning and shaved closely. He wore thick, horn-rimmed glasses. Despite the warm summer day, he wore corduroy pants and cowboy boots. He was slightly built and several inches taller than I. His white, long-sleeved shirt had embroidered appliqués down the front and needed ironing and a little bleach. Nothing was appealing about him—he was a typical "good ol' boy" and not the kind of person I would choose for a boyfriend.

"Interesting belt buckle," I said.

"It's an authentic Navajo buckle. It's solid silver, and the turquoise is very high quality," he said proudly. "Hey, do ya wanna take a ride to see my apartment after we eat? Or you could come over one day next week if you'd rather do that. I want to give ya a tour of my bowling alley. It's not as polished as Iceland Bowl... You have that place running like a well-oiled machine!"

"Well, I am a professional," I said, laughing. "And I don't have a car or a driver's license."

"Ya don't drive? How have you survived, girl?"

"I walk or ride my bike."

"Well then, I'll have to give ya driving lessons!" Jess offered. "How old are ya anyway?"

"Twenty-five... How old are you?"

He hesitated before he spoke. "I'm forty-five."

The age gap didn't shock me; it was the same as my parents'.

After our picnic lunch, we headed to his car. Jess opened the driver's side door and told me to get behind the wheel.

"Why haven't ya got your license yet, girl? Are ya scared to drive?" he asked.

"I'm not afraid! I just haven't had any reason to drive."

"Well, ya must have been living under a rock!"

I couldn't admit to him that, until recently, I was living under a rock. I wasn't allowed to drive, and my father escorted me everywhere.

He explained the gas pedal, brake, clutch, and mirror adjustments. He clarified the dashboard gauges, which seemed like a different language. My head was spinning.

"First gear is number one. To shift to second gear, depress the clutch and pull straight back. Then, depress the clutch again and shift up to the right for third gear, clutch in and pull straight back for fourth gear, and clutch again and shift up to the right for fifth gear."

"What is the 'R' for?"

"Reverse."

He got into the passenger seat. "Clutch in and foot on the brake… now put it in reverse, take your foot off the brake, and give it a little gas."

"The first thing you want me to do is drive backward!" I whined.

"You can do this, Danielle." His faith in me was unwarranted, but I did as I was told. Our heads jerked several times as I attempted to get the car into gear. Jess stayed calm while I was a nervous wreck.

"I think I have whiplash!" I stated.

"Don't worry, you'll get this, girl. Now put it in first gear," he calmly directed. The car jerked and sputtered.

"I'm going to break your car!" I cried out.

"How about you get out, and I'll drive us to a cemetery, and we'll try again? That way, you won't kill anyone," he laughed. We got out of the car and switched seats. He instructed me for the next hour, and I knew at that moment I had never met a man with more patience.

After that, Jess and I started spending much of our free time together. He introduced me to his friends as his girlfriend, and I introduced him as my boyfriend. One of my co-workers asked me if I thought he was too old for me. I laughed. His age didn't matter. Jess treated me respectfully, something I hadn't found with men my age.

Since our first date, he only kissed me on the cheek. One evening, we went line dancing, and things began to change. When we entered the bar, he draped his arm around me, pulled my stool close to his, leaned in, and kissed my lips.

"I hope that was okay with you?" He looked hopeful as he awaited my reply. I felt my heart soften.

"That was nice," I smiled, but my mother's words suddenly echoed in my mind... *Stay single if possible. That way, you'll never have to answer to anyone.*

I followed him into his world and allowed him to take the reins in our relationship. After all, he was older and had many interests beyond work. He introduced me to casinos and taught me how to play blackjack. We went camping, joined a couples' bowling league, and I became a member of the Eagles Club to which he belonged. My life was filled with activities, all of which revolved around Jess.

Jess's kids spent every other weekend with him, and we took them on camping trips whenever the weather cooperated. With his red hair and freckles, Lance followed me everywhere I went and talked constantly, almost as if he craved attention. Sharlee had a smart mouth, as I assumed many teenage girls did, and she had a habit of running away for days at a time if something didn't go her way. Jess was soft on her, and I couldn't help but notice the difference from how I was raised.

I wanted to influence Jess's kids positively and treat them respectfully and kindly. But my makeup, jewelry, and clothing began disappearing every time the kids visited. Money went missing from my purse. More items vanished with every visit, and there was only one explanation: one or both of Jess's kids were stealing from us.

I talked to Jess about the problem, but he didn't take it seriously.

"She's just a kid!" Jess replied when I voiced my suspicions.

From then on, I got into the habit of locking everything of value in the trunk of my car when his kids visited and kept the key in my pocket.

On weekends when Jess didn't have his kids, we followed our favorite band, The Cowboys, from town to town. Jess taught me to line dance, waltz, tango, foxtrot, and quickstep. Before that, the only way I danced was to 80s rock. He said that young people had lost the art of dancing, and I had to agree. I loved the feeling of his arm around me and the way the crowd of dancers moved aside and made room for us on the dance floor.

He was a mature man and didn't add any drama to our relationship that men my age seemed to bring. I felt safe with Jess, and as my feelings for him deepened, he began to look handsome to me.

While we were at a bar one night, he turned to me.

"Danielle, what do ya think about us gettin' hitched?"

We had been dating for a few months, and our lives were woven together. We had much in common, but I felt more like his friend most of the time. We occasionally slept together, but intimacy was always my idea; my hormones were those of a typical twenty-seven-year-old. He had taught me to drive and dance. I felt safe with him. His kids liked me. What more could a girl want?

We talked constantly. I spoke to Jess more than I'd ever talked to anyone besides my sister. But there was something I could not yet bring myself to tell him.

The memory of what my father did had been shelved away as if it had happened to an actress in a movie. I felt sorry for the actress. She couldn't escape; she was held captive, and her every move was monitored. She had no sense of identity or idea that she could live in a different world. She was unaware that help was available. She couldn't tell her mother what was happening because it would upset her. The actress woke every morning and did as she was told. Every day was the same. She was not a person but an extension of the man who ruled her. If she had any control, she was not aware of it.

The movie's audience wanted to scream, "Get away from him!" "Just leave!" "What the hell is wrong with you?!" But she couldn't hear them. It was only a movie, and she was only playing her part—she had no choice but to follow the script.

"Oh, Jess!" I threw my arms around his neck, but my thoughts swirled... *Do I have to tell him? He will never look at me the same way. He will ask questions. He'll know I'm pretending to be normal and that I'm a fraud. He'll be disgusted. I'm damaged. He won't love me anymore...*

"Danielle, I love ya, girl. What do ya say?"

"I say that I love you, too! And, yes, let's get hitched!"

By keeping my secret, was I lying by omission? I had told him bits and pieces about my childhood. I discussed the ranch and how Karole and I cared for the horses. I mentioned the blue ribbon I won in the spelling bee in second grade. When he asked me where I went to school, I said I couldn't recall the names of all the schools.

I read hundreds of books as a child—more than most kids my age. As an adult, my sister's husband taught me math. I didn't think my lack of education was apparent—at least, it wasn't to Jess. I was self-taught and functioned better than most.

I looked forward to my weekly Sunday morning phone call with my mother. I was grateful that my father never answered the phone. During our calls, I would talk about my job and what I was doing with my apartment, while she would tell me about the neighbors and what she was making for dinner. I didn't offer details about my dating life, and she didn't say much about my father.

That Sunday, I called my mother to share the news of my upcoming nuptials. I wanted her to be the first to know. I didn't expect her to be excited, and she did not disappoint. In her defense, she had never met Jess, and I had not given her any details about him. All she knew was his name and age. She suggested we come to dinner so she and my father could meet him.

Karole worked full-time and spent her evenings with her husband. Despite our time constraints, we always found a way to have daily phone calls during our lunch breaks. We kept each other updated on our goings-on but avoided discussing our father. It was almost as if he never existed.

During my lunch break the following Monday, I closed the door to my office. I hesitated to dial, but it would have been unusual if I didn't call. I wanted Karole to be happy that Jess and I were engaged, but I had doubts.

"Hi, sis," she answered. "What's up?"

"Are you sitting down? I have big news, Karole!"

"I'm sitting! What is it?"

"Jess and I… We are engaged to be married!"

"Danielle, I'm happy for you!" she answered with feigned enthusiasm.

"What's wrong, Karole?"

"It's nothing… If you're happy, then I'm happy."

Moments went by without speaking. I didn't want to start a fight, but her opinion was important.

"What are you thinking, Karole? Please tell me."

"You won't like what I have to say," she stated firmly.

"Say it anyway."

She and Phil had met Jess on more than one occasion. They met us for line dancing several times, and we always had a great time.

"Okay… Danielle… Jess is an old man. He's a nice guy, but can he even get it up anymore?"

"Yes! He can get it up!" I was annoyed. I was very aware of the difference in our ages. I would not tell her that sex with Jess was lukewarm or that he had almost no interest in doing it. "Jess loves me; he treats me like a queen. I appreciate his maturity, Karole!"

"Do you love him?" she asked bluntly.

"Yes, I love him!" I protested. "And Daddy is twenty years older than Ma!"

"And look how well that turned out!" she replied sarcastically. Again, moments passed in silence as I gathered the words to explain why this was right.

"Jess loves me, and I love him," I said softly. "We will make it work. He isn't like our father—he's the opposite."

"Then I'm happy for you, Danielle. I only want what's best for you."

"Thank you," I replied. "But…" My voice trailed off as I lost my nerve.

"But what?" she asked.

"Karole… I never told him…"

"You never told Jess about our perverted father? Maybe it's none of Jess's business."

I sensed her anger at that moment—not at me—at the world.

"Have you told Phil?"

"No way," she said calmly. "That's ancient history."

"Don't you think you owe him the truth?"

"No, I don't. Phil would want to kill the bastard," she said as casually as if she had just told me it was starting to rain.

"Are you afraid he won't love you if you tell him?" I asked sheepishly.

"Of course, he'd still love me! Danielle! Why wouldn't he love me? Is that what you're afraid of? That Jess won't love you anymore? That's absurd! We were children, and our father is a sick fuck! Tell Jess if you want—that's your call."

I had to be honest with Jess. He always showed me transparency, and I wanted our marriage to start on a foundation of truth. If he accepted my past and still wanted to marry me, it would assure me that he was the right man for me.

SEVENTEEN

Albuquerque

1984-85

"HOW OLD IS your mother, Danielle?"

"She's fifty-two. Why do you ask?"

"She's not much older than me," he said, concerned.

"Jess, I'm not worried about our age difference, so you shouldn't be either. My mother married an older man, too."

"Did their age difference cause trouble in their marriage?" he asked.

"She made it work. My mother was raised Catholic and believes marriage is for life, as I do!"

He seemed satisfied with my answer.

"Jess," I added, "I don't have a good relationship with my father."

"Why not?"

"It's hard to explain. I will someday, but we're almost there, and I don't have time. I just thought you should know."

"I'm sorry to hear that, but I figured your family wasn't right. After all, you moved from town to town all your life. Something was very wrong with that…"

"When I figure out why we did that, you'll be the first to know," I sighed.

My mother opened the door to let us in. The smell of pot roast wafted from the kitchen.

"Ma, something smells good!" I said cheerfully. She was solemn as she took our coats, almost as if we had just arrived at a funeral. My father was sitting in the living room, smoking a cigarette. I hadn't seen him in a while. He had put on weight and had aged appreciably. He grunted as he pushed himself out of the recliner.

"Daddy and Ma, this is Jess… my fiancé. Jess, I'd like you to meet my parents." I paused as I recalled the names they were currently using… "Raymond and Theresa Watson."

My father and Jess shook hands, but my mother turned and excused herself to the kitchen, mumbling about mashing potatoes and a Jello mold.

"Sit down, Jess," my father said as he fell back into his recliner. I sat on the couch beside Jess and wove my arm through his.

"So… do you hunt or fish?" my father asked. I knew that his list of twenty questions had just begun.

"No sir, I don't do much of either." Jess pulled a pack of cigars from his pocket. "Would you care for a Cuban, sir?" Jess came prepared to make a good impression.

"I don't mind if I do. I always say, 'If you got 'em, smoke 'em.'" Jess lit my father's cigar and sat back down beside me.

"So tell me, Jess… What do you do for a living?"

"I manage the Ranchero Bowl in Rio Rancho," Jess answered. "I basically do the same thing that Danielle does."

"Just how old are you?" my father asked as he studied his cigar.

"I'm forty-six, sir," Jess answered nervously.

"And you want to marry Danielle?" he asked.

"Yes, sir. I love your daughter."

"Do you make a decent wage at Ranchero Bowl?"

"Yes, sir. I pay child support and alimony, but I have more than enough money to cover the rent."

"Ex-wife, huh?" He took another long drag and then exhaled a cloud of smoke in Jess's direction.

"Yes, sir. I have two children from my first marriage."

He turned his attention to me. "Are you ready to take on the role of a stepmother, Danielle?" he asked with a hint of distaste.

Why was he judging us so harshly? What right did he have to act superior? And what was taking my mother so long to call us to the dinner table?

"Daddy, I met Jess's kids. They are good kids, and they love me!"

"What about having a kid of your own? How will that work when your husband is twenty years older than you and has no money because he's supporting his first family?"

"Daddy… Jess had a vasectomy. We won't have children, and I'm fine with that!"

"You're fine with that, huh?" he methodically flicked the cigar into an ashtray. "What if your mother and I want grandchildren?"

I didn't know how to answer the question. Jess nervously puffed away, but no cigar was long enough to relieve his tension.

"Dinner is ready," my mother finally announced from the dining room.

My father sat across from Jess, and the interrogation continued... "Why did you divorce your first wife?" "How old are your children?" "How often do your children visit?" "Are you in good health?" "Do you have money in the bank?"

I ate silently, hoping my father would soon be satisfied and we could focus on something more positive—like our wedding plans. Halfway through the meal, all my mother contributed was, "Pass the gravy."

"Your mother and I are moving to Boise next month."

"Where is Boise?"

"It's in Idaho. Do you know where Idaho is, Danielle?" he said condescendingly.

"Yes, I do, Daddy," I said mid-swallow. I held back from asking why they were moving again or what surname they would use in Idaho.

"So, Jess," my father continued. "Do you see yourself advancing in this career at the bowling alley? Or are you content with the job you have?"

"Well, sir, it pays the bills. What more can I say?"

"You can say that you are trying to better yourself. After all, you *are* marrying my daughter!"

"You don't have to worry, sir. I will take care of your daughter. You have my word on that," Jess said with sincerity.

"You can drop the sir stuff," my father said, irritated. "You are far too old for that. You can address me as Ray."

"Have you set a date for the wedding?" My mother nervously interjected. The tension in the air was thick and getting thicker.

"We are thinking of eloping to Reno. We want a simple wedding," I said.

"Reno!" my father exclaimed. "Isn't that where people go to gamble?"

"Yes, Daddy. People gamble in Reno." He was wearing me down. Since we arrived, every word from his mouth had negative intonations.

"Are you a gambler, Jess?" my father locked his eyes on Jess's face.

"I gamble some," Jess choked out.

"Some? Hmmm." My father didn't buy it. He acted as judge and jury, determining that Jess was too old for me, lacked ambition, and was irresponsible with money.

"I made an apple pie for dessert!" my mother chirped, trying to break the sour mood in the room.

"My mother makes the best pies!" I said as I leaned toward Jess. He looked like he wanted to run out of the house. I put my hand on his hand to reassure him.

"Ma, I have an idea!" I said enthusiastically. Why don't you and Daddy come to Reno with us?"

My father started to cough as if he had swallowed a fly.

"Are you all right?" my mother asked. He held his hand up to stop further questioning.

Jess jerked his head to look at me. I hadn't discussed this with him beforehand, and my impulsive idea blindsided him.

The thought of having my mother at our wedding made me happy, but after asking, I realized the penance I'd pay for my mother's presence. Jess and my father were not getting along... *What was I thinking?*

"I'll have to get back to you about that, Danielle," she said after my father composed himself. "Your father hasn't been feeling well, so a trip to Reno may not work for us," she said smoothly. Making excuses for my father had become as easy for her as breathing.

I looked at her sadly, but I felt relieved. She sensed that my invitation had yet to be thought through.

"Do you golf, Jess?" my father asked as my mother served the pie. He was determined to find out what made Jess tick.

"No, sir... I mean, Ray."

My father shook his head in disbelief. "What the hell do you do besides work and gamble?"

Jess stood up. "Danielle, I think it's time for us to leave." He had had enough. He had been doing his best to remain composed but was losing it.

"Please, Jess, sit down," I said, my eyes pleading. My mother had worked so hard to make the meal, and I didn't want to disappoint her with a dramatic ending to the evening. He reluctantly sat down, and I placed my hand on his knee.

After dessert, my father and Jess returned to the living room for a brandy and another cigar while my mother and I cleared the table. She was reticent as we washed the dishes, speaking only of the weather.

"Ma… Do you like Jess?" I asked in a child-like voice, desperate for approval.

"Do *you* like him?" She did not believe my affection for him was genuine.

"Ma… He's so good to me. I love him!"

"He's twenty years older than you."

"Daddy is twenty years older than you!"

She turned to look at me but said nothing. She didn't have to—I could read her eyes.

"We will make our marriage work. He is teaching me to drive, and he takes me out dancing. He opens doors for me and treats me like a queen. He loves me!"

"It sounds to me like your mind is made up. This is your decision, Danielle, not mine."

I hated that she disapproved, but there was nothing else I could say. It *was* my decision. I was tired of being alone, tired of the immature men I dated, tired of wolf whistles and flirtatious men who all wanted one thing from me. A wedding ring on my finger would put an end to the nonsense.

"Ma… Nobody is perfect. There are probably things about me that Jess doesn't like either." I tried hard to justify my decision to marry Jess, but my mother was not buying it.

"It's your life," she said as she continued to wash the dishes. "Danielle… Next week, your father and I are filing for divorce," she added casually.

"What?!"

"We are only doing it so that when he passes, I will be able to collect widow's benefits from the government. We will remarry as Alouise and Theresa Parise."

"Oh… Is that Daddy's real name?" I asked.

"That is the name he used when he served in the U.S. Army," she answered flatly as if the subject were not unusual.

"Daddy served in the U.S. Army? I thought he served in the Canadian Army."

"He served in both," Mother stated with irritation. I sensed she was uncomfortable with the conversation.

"Is that why you're moving to Boise?"

"That's part of it." She offered no further information.

"Danielle!" Jess called from the living room. "It's getting late. We both have work in the morning."

"I'll finish up here myself," my mother said as she took the dish towel from my hands. "Go. Your fiancé is calling you."

When we walked through the living room, my father stared at the TV and didn't acknowledge that we were leaving. I knew his silence was meant to show his disapproval of my choice of husband. I retrieved our coats, and we left.

"Oh my God! Your father is a horrible person! I can see why ya don't like him. He was torturing me while you were in the kitchen with your mother. He was interrogating me about my children.... How often do I see them? How old is my daughter? How much time do they spend with me? Why did you leave me alone with him, Danielle? And what business is it of his that I had a vasectomy! Why did you tell him that? That is *our* business, not your parents'! I am so glad meeting your parents is behind us! I can die a happy man if I never see your father again!"

I had never seen Jess upset. He had lost all composure.

I felt upset, too. While I didn't care that my father disapproved of him, my mother also had reservations. I wouldn't confess that to him.

"You asked them to come to Reno with us? Why did ya do that, Danielle?! What were ya thinking?!"

"I doubt they'll come… But I wish my mother would come with us and leave him home. We need a witness, right?"

He stopped the car in front of my apartment.

"Are you coming in?" I asked.

"No, I've got to get up early tomorrow. I need to sleep in my own bed."

He leaned over and kissed my cheek. His days of passion were behind him. Another woman had experienced his interest in intimacy, and I was trying to accept that.

EIGHTEEN

Reno

1985

WE DECIDED I would move into Jess's apartment and give up my own. His apartment was more convenient for his job and kids. The downside was that I would have to commute twenty miles to work. Marriage involves compromise, and I was contributing my share.

One by one, I meticulously wrapped the items I bought to decorate my apartment, wondering where they might find a place in Jess's cluttered apartment.

I voiced my concern that we didn't have enough money for the hotel room and other wedding expenses.

"If we just go to the courthouse, we can get married by the Justice of the Peace for the cost of a wedding license," I explained. I was efficient with money, and I wanted Jess to see my point of view.

"But Reno would be fun, Danielle! Let's stick to our plan!" Jess insisted. "I'll go to the bank to get a loan."

Jess tried to get a loan, but his low credit score was an obstacle. In contrast, I obtained a loan quickly with my good credit rating. While I was concerned about the monthly payments due over the next two years, Jess assured me he would cover half the cost. Although paying child support cut into his salary, he reminded me that he had only six years left until his youngest turned eighteen. He promised that living together and pooling our finances would save us a significant amount for our future and help us afford to buy our own home someday.

I suggested that we limit our gambling expenses, and then we argued for days about what the limit should be. I suggested one hundred dollars, but Jess insisted on two hundred. He was confident that he could win big at the blackjack table.

We decided to forgo buying new clothing for the wedding ceremony and get married in blue jeans. We were not fancy people, and as Jess said, "We will be just as married in blue jeans as we would be in a tuxedo and a fancy white dress."

Our future appeared bright, yet I hadn't revealed my secret to him, leaving me shadowed by dread. I couldn't go through with marrying Jess without disclosing the truth about my past, and I feared he might cancel the wedding upon learning it.

Jess stirred pasta in a pot one evening as he prepared our dinner. "Mountain Music" by Alabama was playing on the radio, and he was singing along. When I entered the kitchen, he did a silly two-step dance that made me laugh. He looked so happy, but there would never be an easier time to do what I had to do.

"Jess," I choked out. "Please, sit down?"

"What's wrong, Danielle?" He switched off the radio. The sudden silence left a gap I would fill with unwelcome words.

I was about to ruin his happiness and put our future at risk. My cheeks felt taut; my lips refused to budge. The color drained from my face.

We sat at the kitchen table, facing each other. His expression went blank; he had no idea what was happening inside my head. In the last few months, I hadn't given him any hint of what I had lived through. In conversations, I carefully navigated my memories, sharing only those I could portray as joyful and ordinary.

"Oh my God, Danielle... Are ya calling off the wedding?"

"No! But *you* might want to after I tell you something."

"What are ya getting at, girl? What's so horrible? You're white as a sheet."

I often thought about how to explain the situation to him, but I could never find the right words. Even now, I felt lost; the perfect words didn't exist. I took a deep breath.

"Do you remember I told you how my family relocated constantly and that my father changed our identity in every town?"

"Yeah, what the hell was that about?" He seemed relieved, thinking this was the topic I wanted to discuss. But this was just the beginning of my story—I was gradually easing him into it.

"I don't know why my parents did that. There is more..." I felt overwhelmed and couldn't continue.

"Danielle... Nothin' ya can say will change the fact that I love ya, girl!"

I buried my face in my hands to make my problems disappear. Jess gently took my hands and lowered them to the table.

"Do you remember when I mentioned that I couldn't recall the names of the schools I attended?"

"Yeah."

"That's because the schools didn't exist. I only attended first and second grade. After that…" I paused.

"After that, what?" He had a puzzled expression on his face. "Ya didn't go to school?"

"Karole and I weren't allowed to go to school."

"I'm confused, Danielle, but ya shouldn't have kept this from me. You're an intelligent girl! You balance the books at your job as well as any accountant could. Who taught ya how to do that?"

"Karole's husband, Phil, did. He taught me basic math."

"Why weren't ya allowed to go to school?"

"I think my father was 'on the run.'" I made quotes in the air. "He was paranoid and seemed to think someone was looking for us."

"Is he crazy?"

"There's more…" Jess leaned back in the chair with a look of disbelief. "Karole and I were kept hidden for most of our childhood, and we grew up with a constantly changing identity. My last name changed multiple times as we moved from town to town. In the second grade, I was Danielle Bouchard. I loved being Danielle Bouchard and could have happily remained Danielle Bouchard forever. But after we left Manotick, my last name changed many times. Sometimes, I didn't bother memorizing my new last name."

"What do ya mean by 'You were kept hidden?' Who were ya hidden from?"

"We were hidden from the world. When we lived on the ranch in Athabaska, we were allowed outside, but only to care for the horses and run the ranch. We received clear instructions on the topics we were allowed to discuss with our customers. It stressed me out when strangers asked me my name. I feared I'd say the wrong name, so I often froze and didn't speak. If my mother weren't near to speak for me, I would run away rather than risk saying the wrong name. But once we left Athabaska, we were rarely allowed to go outside."

"I can't imagine a worse childhood." Jess reached for my hands, giving me the strength to continue.

"We hid in the house all day. Sometimes, we were allowed outside, but only when the other kids in the neighborhood came home from school. We were forbidden to tell anyone we didn't go to school, and sometimes we lied and told other kids that we went to a different school."

Jess stared at me with his mouth agape, trying to comprehend the magnitude of what I was telling him.

"Once, Karole became friendly with one of the regular customers and told him how we changed our identity from one town to the next. The man then asked my father why he did that, and the next thing I knew, he sold the horses, gave our dogs away, and we left the ranch."

"I want to wring your father's neck!"

I slid my hands from his and once again covered my face. "There's more," I whispered through my fingers.

Besides Karole, I had never told anyone my secret. Since running away from home, I lived as if nothing unusual happened. I was a fake, an imposter. I wasn't smart; I was only pretending to be smart, and I fooled everyone.

I began to rock back and forth in my seat. *He will never touch me again after he knows the truth. Why did I agree to marry him? Why did I give up my apartment? I'm so stupid.*

"Stupid, stupid, stupid," I said as I rocked back and forth.

"Danielle! Stop saying that! You're a smart girl. Talk to me!"

My thoughts were swimming…

I was fifteen again. I was sitting on the forest floor… He was on top of me… hot breath… stale cigarettes… rough whiskers. He was so heavy. I couldn't breathe. He pulled at my clothing. Then pain… so much pain…

"No! I can't!" I cried into my hands.

After I tell him, every good thing in my life will disappear… I will return to my pretend world, where I am the confident manager who tells everyone what to do and how to do it.

He reached up and again took my hands into his. I looked at him, piercing his eyes, hoping he could read my soul. That way, nothing would have to be put into words. He would understand. He would know I had been a puppet who couldn't think for herself. But that kind of communication didn't exist in this world—maybe the next.

I took a deep breath. *God, please help me.*

"My father… He abused me… He abused us… Karole and me."

"He beat you?" Jess gasped, and his eyes widened in horror.

"No... He *abused* us," I emphasized the word "abused."

Jess's face tightened as if he were preventing himself from becoming sick.

"Do you mean sexually?" The words left his lips as if they were vile, as though he were repeating something the devil had whispered in his ear.

"Yes."

He let go of my hands.

If I could have cried, he might have seen me as an average person with normal human emotions. But my eyes were dry.

My instinct was to run into the bedroom and close the door. I wanted to curl up on the bed with a stack of books my mother had gotten from the library and read for days. I desired nothing more than to immerse myself in someone else's story. Then, I wouldn't have to feel the knot in my stomach that twisted tighter by the minute.

"Did it happen just once?" He jumped to his feet and began to pace.

"No."

"How many times, Danielle?"

"I don't know…" I did not want to lie, but I couldn't admit that the abuse happened regularly.

"More than five times?"

"Yes."

"More than ten times?"

"Yes."

"Oh my God, Danielle! Didn't ya fight him? Didn't ya tell him to stop?"

"Of course, I tried to stop him! He was powerful! Don't forget, he was a professional wrestler."

"Did ya tell your mother?"

"No!"

"Why the hell not?"

"It would have killed her."

"How old were you the last time he raped you?"

"I'm not sure. It wasn't as often once he turned sixty." My answer sounded inconceivable, even to myself.

"Your father is a fucking pervert! Why didn't ya go for help?!"

"I didn't trust the police… I believed the authorities had been chasing us all my life."

Jess shook his head, trying to take it all in.

"This is horrible. Danielle, what your parents did to you is unforgivable."

"My mother had nothing to do with this!" I protested.

"She *must* have known what was going on."

"She didn't!"

"Danielle, do ya really believe that?"

"The truth would have caused her pain. She believes you marry for life. Karole and I knew that, so we kept our secret. What would telling her have achieved?" I argued.

In my eyes, my mother was an angel… a gift sent to me from Heaven. She raised me the best she could under the circumstances. She didn't deserve to suffer because of one mistake… marrying my father. I would never stop defending her; nothing Jess could say would persuade me differently.

"I wrote something about her. I'll read it to you. Then you may understand the love I have for my mother." I ran to our bedroom, found the poem tucked at the bottom of a drawer, and sat at the table again.

"Please, Jess, sit back down."

I cleared my throat and began to read…

"The little girl said to God, 'I'm scared. Where are you sending me?'

God replied, 'Don't be afraid. I will always be with you.'

'But I'm so small. Why can't I stay with you? Did I anger you? Don't you want me to stay?'

God replied, 'Little girl, someone special awaits you. Like an angel, she will love and care for you and teach you many things. She is your mother. But most of all, she will put you on the path that will bring you back to me. Now hush, little girl, it's time to meet your mother.'"

I laid the poem on my lap and looked up for Jess's reaction, sure that he would now understand the depth of my love for my mother after hearing the words from my heart.

"Danielle, why would God place you in harm's way? God gives us all free will, and your parents choose to make terrible decisions. Believe what you want, girl, but I think your mother is as guilty as your father."

"No, she isn't!"

"I don't understand how ya can even walk into their house. The day you introduced me to them, he acted like an asshole, but I didn't have a clue that he was a pervert. I would have never gone there knowing what I know now. But it looks to me like God is already punishing that bastard for what he did. He can barely get his fat ass out of the chair!"

"I want a relationship with my mother, and that's why I tolerate him," my voice cracked.

"Yeah, well, you should be plenty angry with her, too! She's far from the saint that ya paint her out to be. She had to know what was going on, Danielle. As I see it, she pretended to see nothing. Maybe she didn't want to have sex with the creep and turned a blind eye so he'd leave her the fuck alone."

"No! Jess! You've got that all wrong! She would have never put us in harm's way!"

"You once told me that he thought it was funny when he grabbed your and your sister's boobs just as someone snapped a picture... Did your mother see that?"

"Yes."

"And what did she do when that happened?"

"She hated it!"

"But what did she *do* about it, Danielle?"

"She walked away…"

"Danielle… She knew! Your mother knew!"

"Jess, you don't know her like I do. You weren't there. It's complicated."

"Why do you defend her, Danielle? Neither of your parents did what parents are supposed to do."

"What *are* parents supposed to do?" I asked curiously.

"Parents are supposed to keep you safe! And educate you! Your parents failed miserably on both accounts!"

"My mother brought us books to read. So, in a way, she did educate us."

"Danielle..." Jess shook his head in disbelief. He could not see the situation from my viewpoint.

"She tried hard to do the right thing," I answered sincerely. "But oddly, my mother loved me more than she loved Karole, and my father loved Karole more than he loved me. I never understood that."

"I think I do," Jess smirked. "Think about it... He was probably abusing your sister for a long time. Your mother was jealous of the attention he gave Karole... Karole was competition. That's really fucked up."

"When Karole got older, he took her on business trips," I continued to explain. "Every time they returned home, Karole had new dresses, shoes, purses, jewelry..."

"Damn, your poor sister. She got it worse than you did."

"My mother would get angry at Karole and blame her for encouraging my father to spend money on her. I was immature, and I agreed with my mother. I thought Karole used her charms to manipulate him into buying her whatever she wanted. I was jealous of her pretty things."

"He was rewarding her, Danielle. It's as plain as the nose on your face. Only God knows when he started to abuse her." He shook his head in disgust.

"Then he started to take *me* on trips... And he began to buy gifts for me. That's when I realized I was wrong to blame Karole for the gifts he bought her."

"I want to kill him," Jess whispered under his breath.

"What? No!"

"Tell me one good reason why I shouldn't! He doesn't deserve to live! They should both be thrown in jail!"

He got up from the table and started toward the door.

"Jess, no!" I screamed and ran after him. "He might look like an old man, but he's strong! You've got to believe me! He's got guns in the house. He will kill you!"

"Let go of me!" he ordered. "Someone needs to confront that sick fuck!"

"Jess, no! Please come back. He's sorry for what he's done! Violence won't solve anything!"

"Did he apologize to you and your sister?"

"No… But I know he's sorry!"

"Danielle, you are fooling yourself. He's not sorry! I'm going to the police!"

"Jess!" I pleaded, then put my arms around him and hung onto him with every ounce of my strength. "I don't want my mother to know! It will kill her! She will cry the rest of her life!"

Jess began to calm down. I walked him to the couch and sat beside him. He looked devastated. The conversation was unlike anything he'd ever heard before. And it was with me… his fiancé—the girl he would marry in a few weeks.

"Jess… Do you still love me?" I whispered. I was afraid to hear his answer. Of course, he wouldn't. I was damaged beyond repair.

"That's a silly question, girl. Of course, I love ya. None of this was your fault. You were a kid and lived under your parent's control, and I believe ya still do in some regards. You should hate your parents for what they did to you. They don't deserve your love. Don't you feel angry? Don't you want to scream in their faces?"

"I hate my father for what he did to me. And I've wished him dead many times. But I would *never* be angry with my mother!"

I refused to back down from my position, but Jess remained convinced that my mother was not blameless, no matter what I said... But she had to be innocent. To believe anything else was unthinkable.

"I have to ask ya... Did ya think this was normal, Danielle? Over the years, did the abuse seem less of a threat to you and more of a duty? Did you accept it?"

"I knew no other way to live. He is my father, and I wanted him to be happy. He would be angry if I didn't comply, and I didn't want to disappoint him."

Jess held me in his arms for a long time, and I felt his tears falling onto my head. I had hurt him, and I knew he would never see me the same way again. My only consolation was that I had to confess my past just once. Jess would soon be the only husband I would ever have. I would never have to explain the horror I lived through to anyone else again. Seeing his reaction as I spoke was almost as painful as the abuse itself. The abuse not only affected my life but also caused pain to the man I love. Would the pain ever end? If my father were to pass away tomorrow, would I finally be free? Could I put it all behind me and never have to think about it again?

"My sweet girl," Jess finally spoke. "Ya don't have a clue how badly he damaged you. I'll help ya through this, girl. I promise, someday, this will all be a bad dream."

We placed our suitcases in the car's trunk and waited for Karole and Phil to arrive. They had decided to go to Reno with us, and I couldn't have been happier. Karole still had strong reservations about our marriage, but I felt that after she spent two days in the car with Jess, she'd get to know him and understand why I loved him.

My mother called a week before to share their plans. I couldn't find the courage to tell Jess about their decision, but the time to hesitate was over.

"Jess, my parents are flying to Reno to meet us."

"What?!"

"When I told my mother about our plans and asked her to join us, I was just being polite, but she discussed it with my father, and they decided to come."

"I don't want your father at our wedding ceremony, Danielle! I don't know how you're going to keep him away, but I don't want that sick fuck looking at us when we take our vows!"

I had no idea how to fulfill his request, but he would soon be my husband, and I wanted to ensure his happiness.

"Your devotion to your mother is beyond me." He shook his head.

"She's my mother, Jess. She means everything to me." I was stubborn and stood firm in my position. "Their plane lands in Reno tomorrow at 2:00 p.m."

Jess's face was red. "This will be the last time I ever want to lay eyes on your father. I am going to avoid the hell out of him in Reno. After this trip, that is it, Danielle. I mean it. You can visit your mother if you want, but I never want to see him again."

"Woohoo! Reno, here we come!" Jess called out as Karole and Phil drove up the driveway. We had one thousand miles ahead of us, and the ride would be cozy with the four of us in the car.

Hours into the trip, Jess announced, "We could stop in Vegas on the way!"

"There's no extra money for another hotel stay," I explained, but Karole and Phil agreed with him; I was outnumbered. We stopped in Vegas long enough for Jess to lose two hundred dollars at the blackjack table and were on our way again.

The second day, Jess flipped on the radio for the final hundred miles, and the four of us sang along to country tunes as we navigated to the Grand Sierra Resort.

We didn't have a scheduled time for our wedding ceremony, as it was a first-come-first-served chapel. At two o'clock the following morning, after having a few too many drinks and gambling away a little too much money, and with my father fast asleep in his hotel room, Jess and I hurried to the chapel with my mother by my side. We exchanged wedding vows and were pronounced "Mr. & Mrs. Jess Minor," with my mother as our witness. It was just the three of us, exactly how I wanted it to be.

NINETEEN

Rio Rancho

1985-86

MY MOTHER CALLED to tell me that she had bought a new car. Her Granada was too old to drive to Boise, so she offered it to me, and I happily accepted. I had obtained my driver's license shortly after Jess and I returned from Reno.

Jess drove us to my parents' house in Madrid and stayed in the car while I walked to the front door. My mother answered, grabbed her jacket and the keys, and we walked over to the side of the house where the Granada was parked.

"Where is Raymond?" I asked with a half-laugh. "Raymond" his current fake name.

"He will use the name Jack when our divorce is final and after we relocate to Boise. Your father isn't feeling well. He's been sick a lot lately," she explained. I studied her face for any sadness, but her expression remained flat.

She opened the door, and I slid in behind the wheel. The car was old and rusty, but I didn't care. She began to explain the car to me.

"It drives well in the snow, and I left a blanket in the backseat just in case you ever get stuck and you're cold. The instruction book is in the glove compartment. There is no spare tire, so you might want to buy one…"

"I'll figure it all out, Ma. I've got Jess to help me. I'm excited to have a car of my own. This is very generous of you!"

"Well, I'm happy to give you it, " she smiled briefly.

She had finished giving me instructions, and we sat in silence. The car was a soundproof booth; I could ask her anything.

"Ma…"

"Yes, Danielle?"

"Why did we always move when Karole and I were kids?"

"That's all in the past," she said abruptly. "You're a married woman now. Focus on your husband."

"I do focus on Jess, Ma. I was just wondering."

My question had irritated her. Whatever she knew, she wasn't about to share.

When we stepped out of the car, I hugged her goodbye. Jess waved to my mother from his car, and she waved back. I wished he could see in her what I saw—the kindest and most loving woman God had ever created.

I spent the remainder of the weekend waxing the car, cleaning the windows, and vacuuming the interior. On Monday morning, I packed my lunch and kissed Jess goodbye.

Jess had been driving me to and from work every morning, but now I had my car! I felt so adult! I started the engine and put the car in gear. I was still nervous about driving on the highways, so I took the side roads from Rio Rancho to Albuquerque. As a new driver, my hands gripped the wheel tightly, and what should have been a thirty-minute drive was taking over an hour. I feared driving fast, and several other drivers honked their horns at me. One driver shook his fist and yelled out his window, "Learn to drive, lady!" But every time I accelerated, I felt a wave of panic build.

Ahead, I saw a stalled car on the side of the road. A mother with several small children was standing on the sidewalk. The hood of her car was up, and steam was rising from the engine. She appeared to be alone, and nobody was stopping to help.

There was a sudden jolt and a crunching noise as my head flew forward. While looking at the stranded family, I crashed into the car in front of me. Both cars pulled over to the side of the road.

"What the hell, lady!" he screamed as he exited his car. "Look at my car!"

"I'm sorry. I was looking at that woman…"

"Exactly! You weren't watching where you were going!"

My hood had flown up and was bent in half. The front bumper was dangling, and green fluid was dripping from the engine.

"Let me see your insurance card," he said gruffly.

"I just got the car two days ago. I haven't had a chance to call an insurance company yet," I said sheepishly.

"Just my luck!" he yelled as he slapped his forehead.

Minutes later, a squad car pulled up behind us. The officer promptly wrote me a ticket and assigned a date to appear in court.

I found the nearest telephone booth and called Jess at work. He was disappointed I had wrecked the car but glad nobody was hurt.

He left work and came to pick me up. On the drive home, it was decided that I would call Iceland Bowl when we got home and resign, and then he would hire me at Ranchero Bowl.

Several positions were available: the shoe rental counter, cleaning, or working at the snack bar. I chose to work at the snack bar.

I always imagined my next career move as a business manager in a larger company. I enjoyed being the person in charge, making quick decisions, and solving every problem that came my way. Over the past two years, I was the "go-to" person. Everyone brought their issues to me. Nothing disconcerted me, and nothing seemed too complicated to handle.

But now, married, I understood the importance of compromise and relinquished my ambition to advance my career.

TWENTY

Redmond

1986

I SENSED THAT the owner of the bowling alley where Jess and I worked did not like him... Something had occurred, yet all I could determine was that the books were inconsistent, and the owner blamed Jess for it.

Jess's brother, Steve, lived in Redmond, Oregon. Steve told him, "You can't swing a dead cat in Redmond without finding a job. It's a modern-day gold mine!"

Since Jess and I married, we struggled to make ends meet. After paying the rent, bills, alimony, and child support, we barely had enough money for groceries and cigarettes.

We both agreed it was time for a fresh start, and Redmond seemed the perfect place to make it happen.

I didn't see Karole very often after I got married. She lived thirty miles away. We both had busy lives, but we talked on the phone nearly every day. She had softened her opinion about my marriage and no longer voiced disapproval. Karole didn't visit our parents and couldn't understand why I did. However, she always had a distant relationship with our mother, which explained her attitude.

My twenty-seventh birthday was approaching, and Karole and I planned an early celebration at a restaurant midway between our homes. While waiting for her to arrive, I pondered how to tell her about our plans to move to Oregon. I had no idea how she would react to the news.

I waved the moment she walked in the door. She was dressed stylishly in jeans, a long red sweater, and slouchy boots. Her thick shoulder-length hair was curly and sprayed into place. I felt lucky to have found a clean pair of jeans and a flannel shirt that morning. Jess and I had been packing for days, and I was behind on the laundry.

"Happy birthday!" Karole happily embraced me and then settled into the booth opposite me. She had gained a few more pounds, and it took some effort for her to get comfortable.

"Thank you! I love your sweater. Is it new?" I asked.

"Yes! Phil picked it out for me," she smiled, obviously still starry-eyed for her husband. She took a small, wrapped box from her purse and set it before me.

"What is this?" I asked.

"It's your present, silly girl!" she said with a grin.

"What can I get you, ladies?" The waitress appeared, holding a notepad and pen.

"I'll take a burger, fries, and a Coke," Karole ordered.

"I'll have the same, but make mine a Diet Coke."

"Well, open it!" Karole was eager. I knew that she had put thought into the gift. Inside the box was a pair of gold heart-shaped earrings.

"They are beautiful, Karole. You shouldn't have spent so much money on me," my voice cracked from the lump in my throat; the weight of having to tell Karole we were leaving was unbearable.

"Danielle… What is wrong?"

"I'm going to put these on right now and never take them off!" I said with forced cheer, but she knew me too well.

"Danielle… What's wrong?" she asked again.

"Jess and I…"

"You're getting a divorce?"

"No."

"Are you pregnant?"

"No! You know Jess had a vasectomy."

"Oh, yeah. And the old guy can't get it up!" she said sarcastically.

"He can get it up!"

"Then what is it?" Karole stared into my eyes. Diversion was no longer an option.

"We have decided to move."

"To where?"

"Redmond, Oregon," I said, trying to sound persuasive.

"Oregon!" she yelled. "You might as well move to the fucking moon!" People in the next booth looked our way.

"Shhh! Karole, please don't yell."

"You are making another mistake, Danielle. First, you gave up a wonderful job and a sweet apartment, and then you married a man old enough to be your father and became a waitress!"

"Karole! I love Jess!"

"You will hate it in Oregon. I'm sure it's beautiful, but you won't have me!"

"I'll call you... every week," I said, trying to persuade her to be happy for me.

"Our phone calls will be long distance. I can't afford that!" she said too loudly.

"I will call *you* then. There are lots of good-paying jobs out there. And I'll come back to visit you. We can write to each other! I'll write you a letter the day we arrive!" I said, trying to sound upbeat.

"You'll be too busy to write," she said, defeated. "When are you leaving?"

"We're leaving tomorrow, on my birthday."

"Oh my God... Is this really what you want, Danielle?"

"Yes, it's what I want. Jess doesn't like his boss, and I don't like waitressing at the bowling alley. We need a fresh start. Please try to be happy for me."

I stuffed my clothes into a suitcase, put makeup into my purse, and prepared six large boxes to donate to charity. Jess had an impressive collection of bowling trophies that would not make the trip. Leaving room in the trunk for our camping equipment was much more critical.

We packed our belongings into Jess's "Hooptie," a very old, rusty black Buick Skylark with a missing rear window. In anticipation of the chill during our drive from Rio Rancho to Redmond, I threw blankets into the car.

"We are gypsies!" Jess laughed as we drove out of Rio Rancho for the last time.

I felt no sadness as we departed from New Mexico. Neither of us had ever been to Redmond before, and in our excitement, we could hardly stop talking about it.

"Steve said there are jobs posted on every street… good-paying jobs!" Jess couldn't hold back his enthusiasm.

Traveling from town to town was in my blood, so I knew what to expect in a new city. There could be rundown hotel rooms or no hotel rooms at all. His brother might have been embellishing, and there could be no jobs. The people in Redmond may be welcoming, but they could also leer at us in disapproval.

We had five hundred dollars between us and still needed to figure out where we would sleep that night. The Hooptie wasn't roadworthy, and we had over 1,200 miles ahead.

"What kind of job will you look for, Danielle?" he asked.

"Whatever pays the best. I can do just about anything." It was true. Presenting myself as a qualified candidate for a job was a skill I was proud of. I might not have received a formal education, but I graduated summa cum laude from the School of Hard Knocks.

"What do ya say, Danielle? Are you ready to drive straight through to Redmond?!" Jess said with the enthusiasm of a child on Christmas morning.

"I'm game if you're game!"

Several hours into our trip, the Hooptie began to jerk and sputter.

"Damn it! We're running hot. It must be the radiator," Jess said in disgust.

Jess got out of the car and popped open the hood. Steam rolled out.

"Danielle!" he yelled. "Get the jug of water out of the trunk."

As he poured water into the radiator, it quickly dripped out. We drove the Hooptie to a gas station a mile down the road.

"I've got a guy who can fix this in the morning," the attendant said. "There is a motel a ways down the road, and if you can wait for my break in an hour, I'll give y'all a lift."

We were only hours into our trip. I had hoped that five hundred dollars would get us to Redmond with money to spare.

"What's this going to cost?" I asked. We were at the station attendant's mercy; there didn't seem to be another service station for miles.

"About a hundred bucks, give or take," the attendant replied.

I had a cooler of sandwiches in the back of the Hooptie. *At least we don't have to spend money on food.*

As we rode to the motel, I noticed the grounds were neglected, so I assumed the rooms would be seedy. The smell of marijuana wafted toward us as we opened the door to the main lobby. The clerk behind the counter appeared to be no older than eighteen, and his greasy hair was grown halfway down his back. Glassy-eyed, he slowly rose from his chair to check us in.

"Is it just the two of you?" he slurred. Memories of the year I lived with Mark quickly came to mind. He used to smoke "weed" before and after work, so our apartment always smelled like it. My mother always stressed that I should not use drugs, so I never participated, even when Mark insisted that I "take just one hit."

"I think I'll run down the street and get a six-pack at that liquor store we passed," Jess said as we walked toward our room.

"We don't have money to waste on beer, Jess!" I scolded.

"Danielle, don't be a party pooper!"

We took our suitcases and the cooler to our room. Jess left and returned shortly with the six-pack.

I did the math... It would cost $100 to fix the radiator, $30 to rent the motel room, and $5 to buy a six-pack of beer.

"Jess, we spent $135 today. We have a long trip ahead. Please avoid any more unnecessary spending," I blurted out.

"Hey, if I wanted to marry my mother, I would have!" Jess snapped back.

"Jess, think about the gas we'll need. We still have a thousand miles to drive!"

"Danielle, I'm not stupid! I know exactly what's ahead of us. Ya need to stop worrying, girl... Here," he said as he popped open a bottle and handed it to me. "Loosen up a little."

"No thanks. I have an empty stomach. I need to eat something first."

"Ya need to relax, girl! Damn, you're wound so tight."

I reluctantly took the bottle and took a big gulp.

Maybe I am too uptight. Relaxing was something I never considered. Unless I was asleep, my thoughts were on my next move, my next plan, getting the job done, and how I would outsmart those around me to achieve my next goal.

I quickly pulled down the bed covers to check for bugs, a trick I had learned while growing up. I was relieved to find none.

I didn't mind how the beer made me feel. My head felt light, and my troubles far less severe. I took another drink, and Jess laughed.

"I think this beer is making me drunk," I laughed.

"Then I think ya need another!" he said as he opened another bottle.

We hauled our suitcases a mile down the highway to the gas station the next day. The mechanic also replaced a couple of hoses and a gasket, bringing the total bill to $150.

"We need a chunk of ice," I informed Jess when we were back on the road. "I don't want our food to spoil."

"Hey, there's a diner up ahead!" Jess pointed.

"Can't we just have a sandwich for breakfast? I made so many!"

"Stop worrying so much about every penny. I'm in the mood for bacon and eggs!"

I scanned the menu, looking for the cheapest breakfast option. The waitress poured our coffee and took our order.

"And, sweetheart," he said to the waitress, "keep the coffee coming, and can ya bring me a piece of that cherry pie you got over there on the counter?" Jess handed the menu back to the waitress. "Do ya want a piece of pie, too, honey?" he asked me.

"No, thank you," I declined.

I discovered something about my husband of one year... He had no idea how to save money. I should have seen this coming. He attributed his lack of funds to the money he paid to his ex-wife every month, but I was beginning to realize there was another cause... He had trouble controlling his spending. I pulled a pen out of my purse and started writing on a napkin. Maybe if I could show him in black and white, he'd be more cautious with our money.

"What are ya writing?"

I slid the napkin around for him to read and began to explain.

"Yesterday, we spent $185, which was not within our budget."

"Ya, well, shit happens, Danielle!"

"I know shit happens. But that is why we must be more careful with the money we have left, Jess. We need to use our money for gas and ice. Eating at restaurants is a luxury. I packed enough food to feed us for the entire trip."

Seeing the numbers seemed to help him understand.

"Okay! Sandwiches for the rest of today!" he agreed.

We drove for fourteen hours without any issues, stopping only for bathroom breaks and gas. When we arrived in Idaho, we pulled into a rest stop. The temperature had dropped to near freezing, and Jess's fingers were nearly frozen to the steering wheel. Even with the car's heater running at full capacity, the lack of a rear window made the heater almost useless.

"We can't drive any further," I said through chattering teeth. "It's too cold, and you need to rest. We only have a few hundred miles to go, and we can do that tomorrow." I wrapped several blankets around him.

"Jess," I asked with my head resting on his shoulder. "Do you miss New Mexico?"

"Well, I miss my kids, of course. You?"

"I miss my sister. She wasn't happy we were leaving. Once we're settled, I'll call her."

We fell asleep mid-conversation under layers of blankets. Hours later, in the black of the night, we heard a sharp tap on our window that startled us awake. It was a police officer. Jess rolled down the window.

"Hello, officer," Jess said in a friendly tone.

"Is everything okay here? I noticed you don't have a rear window in your car. You two must be freezing to death."

"We're fine, officer. The Mrs. and I fell asleep when we stopped to rest!"

The officer leaned down and flashed a light in my face. "Miss... Are you okay?" He gazed at me briefly as if attempting to assess the situation.

"I'm fine," I answered. My heart began to race. I had never spoken to a police officer before. The officer then told us to drive safely and not to forget to wear our seatbelts.

Jess drove out of the rest stop and merged onto the highway. He started to laugh.

"I think he thought you were my daughter!"

"Or your hooker!"

The officer had scared me half to death. He had a gun and handcuffs attached to his belt. My heart was beating wildly.

"I was afraid he was going to arrest us!" I began to breathe rapidly, and I could not stop.

"Whoa, slow down that breathing, girl. You're hyperventilating."

Jess reached over the backseat into the cooler. He took a bag of sandwiches and dumped them out while focusing on the road ahead.

"Hold this over your face and breathe into it," he ordered. I held the bag over my nose and mouth as he instructed. My lungs felt raw.

"In and out, girl… nice and easy… in and out…"

His voice was soothing, and within minutes, I was breathing normally. I was embarrassed; I couldn't explain why I was so afraid of the officer. Or maybe I could.

My father always told my sister and me that the law was "out to get us." He told us *never* to talk to police officers or even make eye contact with them; avoid them at all costs. Why did he instill that fear in my sister and me?

My fear was irrational, but it was deeply ingrained in me. It was part of the "damaged" me—the part of me that stopped maturing from age fifteen to twenty-three.

Besides my sister, I knew of no one else who had been sexually abused. I saw magazine articles about girls who had been molested, but I never read one where the molester had been their biological father.

We slept for hours at the rest stop and were eager to drive the last three hundred miles to Redmond—where we would build a new life together. Maybe it was the town where I could put everything behind me and recreate myself. I had been pretending to be "normal" for some time, but now I wanted to discover genuine normalcy and desperately wanted to live it.

TWENTY-ONE

Redmond To Bend

1986-87

WE DROVE FOR hours through Idaho and saw no signs of civilization. If Hooptie died in this desolate part of the world, we would surely perish.

We finally passed the "Welcome to Redmond" sign.

"We made it, girl!" Jess whooped. "Now, keep your eyes open for a motel."

"I can't wait to take a hot bath! When we have enough money, we're getting that back window replaced!" Even with three blankets wrapped around me, I couldn't feel my fingers or toes.

We spent an hour driving around the small town looking for a motel and finally came across one that advertised "Weekly Rates."

"That will be $140 for the week," the clerk behind the counter said.

"How much money does that leave us with?" Jess asked as we walked with our suitcases toward our room.

"We've got a little over one hundred left," I sighed.

"We'll *have* to find jobs tomorrow!" I wasn't kidding around.

The mildew smell was noticeable as soon as we walked into the room. The walls were covered with dark paneling. The bed had a gaudy floral bedspread and was flanked by two nightstands, each with a brass-tone lamp. The green flat carpet was worn and spotted. Above the bed hung a cheap picture of a pond surrounded by trees. Nicotine-stained gold drapes hung over the window. I pushed the drapes aside and slid the window open. In the far corner of the room was a shelf holding a television, with a small refrigerator directly beneath it. When I pulled back the sheets on the bed, I discovered a spider hiding. I quickly took action and dealt with it.

I had stayed in much worse places; sleeping in the car for weeks came to mind. I would have to make this work, as this would be home for a while.

"Do we have a bathtub?" I called to my husband in the bathroom.

"Yes, but I don't think you'll want to lie in it once you see it."

I peeked into the bathroom to inspect it. The enamel was worn, and cleaning it would require much effort.

"Let's go find a grocery store. I'll buy some cleaning supplies. I will take a hot bath tonight even if I have to do it blindfolded!" I half-laughed.

I wouldn't let something as trivial as a disgusting bathtub ruin our joy. We had arrived safely in Redmond, the Hooptie didn't die again, and we had enough money to buy supplies and groceries. This was a cakewalk compared to some of the things I had lived through.

I set up a temporary kitchen in the corner of the room, arranged our groceries on the shelf next to the TV, cleaned the bathtub, filled it with hot water, and stepped in.

"Jess!" I called out. "There's room for two of us in this tub!"

"I'm watching The Price Is Right!" he replied.

No matter. I lathered myself up and shampooed my hair. I wore it short when we married but let it grow in the past year. Jess liked longer hair.

After breakfast, we hit the streets to find the "Help Wanted" signs that Steve had told us about. We parked our car and walked downtown, passing one establishment after another. By noon, we had found only one "Waitress Wanted" sign at a mom-and-pop diner.

We stopped at a filling station to buy a map of the area, then sat down at a McDonald's to study it. An older, local man stopped at our table and offered to help. Jess asked him where the factories were, and the man was happy to assist. He took a pen from his pocket protector to mark the locations of several factories and wished us luck.

Despite applying for jobs at every conceivable establishment in Redmond, Jess and I could not find employment. The money we arrived with lasted only a week. Saturday came every time we turned around, and the weekly rent for the motel room was due again. To earn money, we collected, cut, and bundled wood to sell to campers for burning in fire pits. We barely made enough to cover the rent, and little money was left for food. The hopeful anticipation we had arrived with turned to despair, and I was beginning to think we were going to starve to death.

I dragged myself out of bed on a cold February morning and threw a blanket over my shoulders. The room was freezing. I felt the radiator, and it, too, was frigid. The office wouldn't open for a few hours, so we would have to deal with the lack of heat until then. Jess was fast asleep. Typically, we woke up at six, and after having coffee and breakfast, we got into the Hooptie to search for work.

A neighbor at the motel received a daily newspaper. Every morning, I would quickly peruse the want ads and return the newspaper to his doorstep before he woke up. That morning, I saw an advertisement for a factory that made saw blades.

"Jess, wake up. I made coffee."

In discouragement, we were beginning to sleep longer and longer. I had to become a cheerleader and boost our morale.

"Jess! Get your butt out of bed! There are new jobs posted today."

I copied the information from the newspaper onto the motel stationery.

"I'm not getting out of bed… This room is too damn cold," he moaned.

"Put a blanket over your shoulders and have coffee with me. Today is going to be the day we find work! I can feel it in my bones!" I exclaimed.

"How can you feel anything in this cold?" he said as he threw the covers over his head and rolled over.

"Jess! Get up! I want to be the first in line when the factory opens!"

He rose from the bed, and I poured his coffee. My eagerness seemed overwhelming, but his apathy was becoming annoying, and I couldn't allow it. My all-too-familiar survival mode was kicking in; we would perish if we continued down this path.

With much urging, we left at 7 a.m. and drove to the first factory on my list. The rear window of our car still needed replacement, but finding money for food and rent was the priority.

Two weeks later, the factory's manager called. My application had been accepted, and they asked if I could start work the following day. I did my best to temper my enthusiasm. They didn't offer Jess a job. I told him the factory probably needed to meet a quota for hiring women, so they hired me instead of him.

With a steady income, we moved out of the motel and into a tiny home. The rent was lower than what we paid at the motel, and we were more than ready to leave the dingy room behind. Jess's mood improved after we moved, and he began looking for work again.

When spring arrived, we drove to Tumalo State Park and pitched our pup tent. We could see the Deschutes River from our campsite and listened to the sounds of the river as we slept. In the morning, we woke up with the birds and crawled out of our sleeping bags to make a pot of coffee on the coals that were still hot from the campfire we had the night before. We watched the sky turn orange to blue as the sun rose over the Cascade Mountains. The air had never smelled so fresh, and I counted my blessings with every breath.

After cooking bacon and eggs on our camp stove, we packed our fishing gear and went to the river. Most mornings, we caught a trout or two and occasionally a salmon. Later that day, we would fry the fish over our campfire in a skillet with sliced potatoes in butter.

The camping destinations seemed endless, and each park was more beautiful than the last. Smith Rock State Park and Skull Hollow were our favorites.

After a year, we had assimilated into the community. We became members of the Eagles Club, where we enjoyed dancing, a delicious dinner, and playing blackjack. I was happier than ever, and I assumed Jess was happy, too. I went to the saw blade factory every weekday morning while Jess bundled and sold wood to campers.

On weekend mornings, I would call my sister or mother. We would chat quickly; even the lower weekend rates could add up. It wasn't the same as talking face-to-face, but I needed to hear their voices.

During one conversation with my mother, she announced that my father had received the Purple Heart Award from the United States Army in the mail.

"Ma… Daddy fought for Canada under the name A. Alfred Aubin; he served in the U.S. Army under the name Alouise Parise, and he married you with the surname Bouchard," I was treading on forbidden soil, but I was thirty years old. Old enough to deserve some answers. "Why did Daddy change his name so often?"

"Curiosity killed the cat," she said sharply, and I knew not to push the subject any further.

She told me that my father rarely got off the couch these days. She said he never felt good anymore. I faked concern. I couldn't have cared less and secretly wished he would disappear. If I ever told her what he did to me, what he did to Karole, maybe she would hold a pillow over his face at night and put an end to his miserable existence.

When Jess and I were camping, sometimes we skipped fishing, drove thirteen miles south to Bend, and treated ourselves to a fast-food restaurant. One morning, while walking in downtown Bend after breakfast at a local diner, we passed Greenwood Bowl and spotted a "Help Wanted" sign in the window. We both had experience managing a bowling alley but decided that Jess should apply. I made decent money at the saw blade factory, and he desperately wanted to quit bundling wood.

Bend was twenty miles from Redmond, making it a considerable commute for Jess. However, the hopeful look on his face made me realize that getting this job would make him happy.

We parked the Hooptie down the road from the bowling alley the following day. We didn't want the bowling alley's owner to see our run-down car. Jess wore brown corduroy pants and an embroidered rodeo shirt with pearl snaps, and I wore my navy blue suit.

We confidently walked into the bowling alley for Jess's 10 a.m. interview with the owner, Larry Cook. Larry came out of his office to greet Jess, and after they shook hands, Jess introduced me.

"Mr. Cook, I'd like you to meet my wife, Danielle. She also has experience working in bowling alleys. She managed Iceland Bowl in Albuquerque, and I managed Ranchero Bowl in Rio Rancho."

The owner's eyes widened, and I sensed that he was impressed. He invited us into his office, and an hour later, he hired both of us.

I couldn't quit the saw blade factory fast enough. My life felt amazing. I was back working in a business I understood and excelled in. Jess and I worked well together and divided our duties. He balanced the books and organized the leagues, while I managed the snack bar, rental shoes, and cleaning staff.

After several months, Larry approached us with a proposition. He said the bowling alley had never run so smoothly and wanted us to live closer. We had already been searching for an apartment in Bend, but the rent was out of our reach. Larry suggested helping us find a house and offered to co-sign the loan. Weeks later, we found a small white house on a tiny lot, and as promised, Larry co-signed the loan.

The house needed repairs. The kitchen cabinets were falling apart, and the old wallpaper needed to be removed. The vinyl floors were loose at the seams and required replacement. The light fixtures were filled with insects, and the refrigerator would need hours of cleaning to be usable. I was prepared for the challenge, but it quickly became apparent that my husband wanted little to do with it.

In the evenings, after washing the dinner dishes, I started working on renovating the kitchen while Jess relaxed on the couch with a beer and a cigarette. Occasionally, I would call for assistance, and he reluctantly came into the kitchen to hold the ladder for me or to hand me a screwdriver. After several weeks, I repaired the cabinets, installed shelf liners, removed the old wallpaper, painted the walls a warm yellow, and secured the loose vinyl flooring.

One evening, the phone rang; it was my mother. She had news: My father and she were moving from Boise to Madras. They wanted to live closer to me, only a thirty-minute drive, and could visit more often. I feigned enthusiasm, knowing my husband would not be happy with the news.

Jess surprised me with a German Shepherd puppy he had found at the local shelter. We named him Danny.

A year flew by in a whirlwind of work, camping trips, line dancing, and blackjack. Our weekends were fully booked, and new friends often invited us to join them.

I kept the house clean, cooked meals, and did laundry. Although I made some progress on the to-do list that hung on the refrigerator, I only accomplished a fraction of what needed to be done. Eventually, I gave up. Without my husband's help, completing the to-do list seemed unachievable.

The upside of my busy life was that I didn't dwell on my past and didn't focus on the bitterness in my heart.

I occasionally drove up to Madras alone, making up an excuse that Jess was working or sick. I enjoyed seeing my mother, and I ignored my father. He was an irritant, someone who had wronged me. He was old and sickly, and I lived for the day when he would take his last breath.

TWENTY-TWO

Bend

1987

I ARRIVED HOME after a long day; Jess greeted me at the door with an odd look.

"Your mother called… The asshole is dead."

"What?"

"Your father is dead," he clarified.

I had imagined this moment a thousand times and thought I would leap with joy, unable to wipe the smile from my face. But when it finally arrived, I froze. I felt nothing—no emotion and not the great wave of relief I had been waiting for.

"What happened?" I asked.

"A blood clot went to his lungs. Your mom said she called an ambulance because he couldn't breathe. She said he was scared, and he suffered."

"He suffered, huh?" I felt little sympathy.

"The bastard is dead, Danielle. It's over. May his soul burn in hell!"

"No!" I cried. "I don't want him to burn in hell!"

"It doesn't matter what *you* want, Danielle. He has to meet his maker. The man was a monster. He raped you and your sister, and I am willing to bet money that he raped other women, and maybe that's one of the reasons you moved all the time. He probably ruined other lives... not just you and your sister's."

I felt the blood drain from my face as I flopped down on the couch. Jess's statement made me feel weak and sick to my stomach. Why had it never occurred to me that my sister and I weren't the only people he abused? By keeping silent to protect my mother, did I allow harm to come to others? I hid my face in my hands. On top of everything I had to deal with, did I also have to bear the guilt of my father ruining the lives of others?

"Why didn't I stop him? This is too much!" I cried.

"You bear zero blame for what happened to you, and don't you dare blame yourself for what he might have done to others!" Jess said sternly.

My chest began heaving uncontrollably. Emotions I had suppressed rose to the surface; I could no longer conceal them. Jess sat next to me and took me in his arms.

I cried for the two little girls who were moved from town to town and couldn't go to school or look out the windows. I cried for my sister; she endured more abuse than I could ever imagine. She may have been a toddler when the abuse started. She was damaged beyond repair, and she would never recover.

I cried for myself, a fifteen-year-old girl whose innocence was stolen in the cruelest way possible—the young girl who took an innocent walk into the woods with her father. And the girl who emerged from the woods as a different person.

Was he grooming me my whole life? Did he have a plan for what to do to me when my sister was no longer at his beck and call? Did he crush my self-esteem every day to keep me in my place? To maintain control over me?

My mother had always sensed his contempt for me. He hated me from the day I was born. She could never convince him that she had not cheated on him with another man. How convenient for him to insist I wasn't his biological child; in that way, in his sick mind, what he did to me was not incestuous.

I wept for the lost years—the most critical years of my life when I should have been developing friendships and dating. During the dark years of abuse, I formed no meaningful relationships other than the bond I shared with my family.

I cried at the memory of fighting to stop him; I was no match for his strength. He would cover my mouth so I would not scream. "*If you tell your mother what we do, it will kill her to know that her own daughter encouraged her father. Do you want to be responsible for killing your mother?*"

"I didn't want to kill my mother!" I cried in my husband's arms. "I would never do anything to hurt her. I had to protect her!"

"I know, Danielle. I know," he said as he stroked my head.

My bedroom door would open in the middle of the night, and he'd climb into my bed without speaking. His hands searched my body as his breath quickened. I turned my face to avoid his, but I could never escape the smell of cigarettes or the roughness of his whiskers. I hated what he did to me, but it was the only time he loved me.

Under his weight, my bed frame would creak rhythmically, and I was terrified the sound would wake my mother. I stared at the door, praying it would not open with my mother on the other side. Please, God, don't let Ma wake up... Don't let her hear the bed squeaking; I prayed every time. By some miracle, the squeaking bed frame never woke her up. My prayers were answered, and I was spared from bearing the responsibility of destroying my family.

When he was through, he sat at the edge of my bed and composed himself.

"You liked it, too, Danielle. Don't deny it."

When he left the room, I reached for a tissue from my nightstand to wipe myself. I lost count of how often he came into my room, but weeks became months, months became years.

I lifted my head and looked into my husband's face. I was exhausted and could cry no more.

"You got my shirt all wet," Jess said with a sympathetic smile.

I felt so lucky to have found this man. Everyone had been wrong. Our age difference didn't matter at all. He knew from the start what he was getting into; I told him my history before we took our vows. He promised to help me through this and was true to his word.

"We have to go to the funeral," I stated. "Ma needs me."

Jess opened his mouth to speak, but knowing my unwavering love for my mother, he decided not to. I knew what he was going to say, but he was wrong.

TWENTY-THREE

Madras

1987

PHIL HELD KAROLE'S hand as they entered the dimly lit room. I hadn't seen my sister in two years and barely recognized her. She had put on even more weight, and walking seemed a struggle.

"Karole!" I yelled too loudly. My mother looked as if to tell me I was being disrespectful. I hurried toward Karole, embraced her, and then hugged Phil. Phil left to sit next to Jess, leaving Karole and me alone.

"Danielle, you look good! I like your hair at this length and love your dress!"

"I found it at Goodwill yesterday," I whispered. It was black with gold buttons running down the front, suitable for a funeral.

"You look good, too! I love your blouse!" She wore black pants and a floral blouse that reached her knees.

"I'm a cow, but I love you for lying."

"Please don't say that! You're beautiful! You've always been the pretty sister." I grabbed her hand.

"Let's do this," I said, leading her toward the front of the room toward the casket. Suddenly, she stopped in her tracks.

"Why are you stopping?" I asked.

"I am close enough to see the bastard is dead," Karole said coldly.

"Please, Karole, walk with me and at least pretend to be sad... for her sake."

"Should we tell her?" Karole said. "He's dead. Maybe it's time she knew what her husband did. Look at her standing there... the devoted wife grieving for her husband. With one sentence from me, she could substitute her grief with anger."

"Karole, no!" my heart began to race. "Not today, please! This isn't the right time."

"When will be the right time, Danielle?" Karole looked at me with longing eyes. I didn't know how to answer her. She suffered greatly at his hands and had earned every right to do whatever was needed to help herself heal. I knew that. But I could not allow it.

"Let's get through this day like a normal family. Please, Karole... If you can't do it for Ma, do it for me."

I cleverly appealed to her protective instincts and prayed she wouldn't make a scene. I pulled her the rest of the way to the casket, and my mother interpreted Karole's hesitation as grief.

The three of us stood silently, staring at my father's body. Karole reached into the casket, touched his hand, and seemed satisfied that it was cold.

I stared down at his face. His eyes sunk into his head, and his skin was leathery and gray. He looked deflated. Nobody said, "He looks asleep," or "He looks so peaceful." He looked like he had fought a battle against evil, and evil had won.

Jess sat toward the back of the room with his arms folded across his chest. He knew what my father had done and didn't want to pretend otherwise.

"He suffered at the end. He was in a lot of pain, and he couldn't breathe," my mother said flatly, not revealing her emotions.

I held my breath, waiting for Karole to say, "I'm glad he suffered." Instead, my sister and I stood mute and let my mother continue.

"He wasn't religious, so I didn't think a service would be necessary."

He had stopped being a threat to me years ago, but the knowing look he gave me lingered until the end. As long as he was alive, he held memories of me, and I felt it every time he looked at me. Now he was dead, and I alone was the keeper of those memories.

I thought I'd be free the moment he took his last breath. But I didn't feel free. I had been waiting for his death all my life, and now that the moment had arrived, I imagined his eyes opening and his head turning to find me.

His entire life, he was a force to be reckoned with. He sucked the air out of any room he walked into. I had witnessed his acts of kindness, but those rare moments were self-serving. If he was kind to anyone, you could be sure he had an ulterior motive. His gifts to my sister and me were to control us. The anniversary and birthday flowers he gave our mother were intended to prove to anyone watching that he was a devoted husband. It was all an act; he did nothing without an agenda.

If he had a soul, where did it go? When he took his last breath, did the devil grab him by the foot and yank him into eternal flames? Or was there a loving angel waiting to take him under his wings to God? Was God happy to see him and said, "I forgive you, my son?" Or was God angry and flung his sorry soul straight to hell?

Only minutes before viewing time was to end, my Aunt Gladys (my father's sister) and cousin Dottie entered. They dutifully viewed my father's body and then turned to my mother.

"Why did Jack die at a hospital in Spokane?" Aunt Gladys asked my mother in just above a whisper.

"It was the nearest VA hospital," my mother answered curtly.

Aunt Gladys then greeted Karole and me with open arms. I had met Aunt Gladys only once when I was young, and I remembered her as cold and standoffish. But now she seemed warm and loving. What had changed over the past twenty or so years? Dottie initially extended her hand but then hugged Karole and me instead.

The funeral director approached my mother. "Mrs. Parise, if your family is through, I will close the casket, and I will see you tomorrow morning at ten o'clock at the VA Cemetery."

As the casket closed, I waited to see if I felt anything, but I felt nothing. Not joy, not sorrow, and nothing in between. I glanced at my sister. She was looking at her watch.

I squinted as we walked into the sunlight from the dark funeral home.

"Aunt Gladys and cousin Dottie will be joining us at my house for lunch," Mother said before getting in her car. She made no effort to hide her distaste for my father's side of the family.

"I have thought of you two girls a million times over the years," Aunt Gladys said with tears as we stood on the front lawn of my mother's house. I wondered why she thought of us a million times. We had never been a part of her life. Did she even know my sister and I existed?

I introduced Jess to my aunt and cousin, and Karole introduced Phil.

My cousin Dottie's attendance at my father's wake puzzled me; she had never known my father. Was she keeping Aunt Gladys company or curious to see her Uncle Jack's family? Did they wonder what kind of woman married him and what his offspring looked like? Were we just a curiosity?

My mother had prepared dinner that morning in anticipation of our relatives' arrival. We gathered around the oblong dining room table, previously set for seven. All eyes lit up as she presented a pot roast with potatoes, a gravy boat, string bean casserole, a green jello mold, and a relish tray. Aunt Gladys offered to say grace before passing the dishes around the table.

It was a scorching summer day, and two fans were pointed at the table. Small talk dominated the conversation, and everyone commented on the heat wave.

"I'd love to hear what you two girls have been up to!" Aunt Gladys said cheerfully. Her eyes shimmered as she spoke. I wished I had known her while growing up. I had never met my paternal grandparents, and Aunt Gladys seemed the next best thing.

"I manage an eyewear store at the mall in Albuquerque," Karole said proudly.

"That sounds very challenging! And Danielle, do you have a job? Or are you a homemaker, dear?" Aunt Gladys asked kindly.

"Jess and I manage a bowling alley in Bend."

"Well, that is also very impressive! You two girls are doing well for yourselves!" Her smile lingered as she looked back and forth between Karole and me. "And, Phil... What do you do for a living?"

"I work at Montgomery Ward, ma'am."

"Well, I am happy that you all are gainfully employed! I've been retired for years now."

"What did you do, Aunt Gladys?" I asked.

"I worked at an insurance company for thirty years," she said proudly. "Theresa... Are you retired, or are you still working?"

"I clean apartments."

"Oh, well, that's nice, dear," Aunt Gladys added sympathetically. "And what did Jack do all day while you cleaned apartments?"

"He fished, and occasionally, he'd go on an excursion around the state."

"Sounds like he had a nice life; God rest his soul," Aunt Gladys said with a hint of disapproval.

"Who has room for strawberry-rhubarb pie and ice cream?" my mother asked.

We each carried a glass of lemonade and a plate of dessert to the front porch. While eating, several neighbors walked past and offered their condolences to my mother. One neighbor said, "I'm so sorry for your loss," then whispered to his wife as they walked away.

My mother and aunt gathered the dessert dishes and disappeared into the kitchen, leaving Karole, Phil, Jess, and me with our cousin, Dottie. I imagined Dottie had questions she wanted to ask Karole and me. We had lived anything but a conventional life and, until today, had disappeared from her life.

"So… Where did you girls grow up?" Dottie asked.

"More like, where *didn't* we grow up!" Karole said sarcastically. "I can't even recall all the places we lived… And he changed our last name in every town," Karole removed a flask from her purse, poured some brandy into her lemonade, then reached over and poured some into Phil's glass.

"Karole," I said under my breath as I threw darts with my eyes. I wanted her to cease sharing our family secrets with our cousin, whom we barely knew.

"We tried to find you guys many times. It was as if you all disappeared off the face of the earth," Dottie said sadly.

"That was by design!" Karole answered with a half-laugh. She did not get my hint to stop talking. I changed the subject.

"I never got to meet our grandparents, Dottie. What were they like?"

"Our grandmother wasn't a very nice person. She caused problems between the three sisters and always pitted one against the other. Grandfather was quiet and barely spoke a word. They died when I was quite young, so I don't remember that much about either one of them. You didn't miss much."

"Dottie, would you like to exchange phone numbers? I'd love to keep in touch," I offered. Dottie seemed like a genuinely lovely person.

"I'd like that!" Dottie answered, and then scribbled her phone number on a napkin.

A while later, the door opened, and my mother and aunt walked onto the porch.

"It has been so nice to see you girls after all these years!" Aunt Gladys exclaimed. "Would you let me take you both out to lunch tomorrow?"

Karole and I agreed to meet my aunt the following day. We settled on a café in downtown Madras, across from the Texaco station. Aunt Gladys did not invite our husbands or my mother, and it was apparent that she wanted to speak to only Karole and me. She was very different from our father, and I could hardly believe they were brother and sister. Aunt Gladys was kind and spoke softly to us, almost as if we were little girls. I wondered if she knew more than she let on.

The next day at lunch, she asked us where we had lived and where we went to school. Karole told her we had relocated a few times but mostly lived in Athabaska, Tennessee, and New Mexico. I said I couldn't remember all the names of the schools we attended.

After lunch, Aunt Gladys asked if she could pray over us to "save our souls." Karole and I looked at each other and then nodded in agreement. I had no idea that my soul needed saving. Aunt Gladys put one hand on my head and the other on Karole's.

"We adore You, oh Christ! By Your holy cross, You have redeemed the world. Christ died for our sins, that He might bring us to God. We have been sanctified through the offering of the body of Jesus Christ!" People in the café were looking our way. I couldn't decide if I was comforted or wanted to hide. "Lord Jesus! Have mercy on their souls!" She said a little too loudly.

My aunt meant well and must have suspected our troubled childhood. She must have sensed something about my father when they were children. She must have known he wasn't right and that he would create chaos wherever he went.

Dottie pulled her car to the curb at the arranged time to pick up Aunt Gladys. Many bags were tossed in the back seat—she had been shopping.

"Danielle!" Dottie waved me over to her side of the car. "My daughter's fiancé works for the CIA. I could ask him to get some details about your father. Maybe he could find out why your family moved so much."

"You don't have to do that. I think my father was just paranoid." I said through the car window.

I watched as they drove away. How interesting… After so many years, my mother reached out to my father's family. Perhaps she believed it was her responsibility to inform them of his passing. Whatever the reason, I encountered my extremely religious aunt and lively cousin, and I was determined not to let our revived relationships fade again.

TWENTY-FOUR

Bend

1988

I TOOK THE early shift that Monday. Jess wasn't a morning person and preferred taking the later shift. I was busy at my desk when Larry entered my office. His serious expression was unusual; he was typically smiling and carefree.

"What time is your husband coming to work today?" he asked.

"He'll be here at four. Is something wrong, Larry?"

"I'll need to talk to the both of you as soon as he gets here."

My stomach twisted. What could be wrong? When he left my office, I closed the door and quickly called Jess.

"Do you know what's going on with Larry? He wants to talk to both of us. He looks upset, and he won't tell me why."

"The books didn't balance last week," Jess stated flatly.

"What do you mean, Jess? It's your job to balance the books." Just then, there was a knock at my door. I put the phone down. A customer complained that he had reserved four lanes for ten o'clock that morning for his daughter's birthday party, and the reservation was not honored. "Jess, I've got to get back to work... I'll see you later." *Click.*

Jess was running thirty minutes late. "I'm sorry," he said when he stuck his head in my office.

"What are you sorry for?" I said, puzzled. Was he sorry for being late? Was he sorry for making a mistake while balancing the books? Within moments, Larry was standing behind Jess.

"Please, sit down," Larry said sternly. He looked shaken as if his world was falling apart. Little did I know that *my* world was about to fall apart. Larry closed the door behind us.

"I'll get right to the point," he said as we sat. "I've been over and over the books. Over half of the money collected in the last three months for the leagues has disappeared, and boxes of our best Cuban cigars have gone mysteriously missing. There is only one explanation... Jess is stealing from me," Larry said while looking at me, awaiting my reaction.

My jaw dropped. *There must be a mistake. Jess wouldn't take money that didn't belong to him!*

Jess stood up and, without a word, walked out of the office.

"You're fired, Jess!" Larry yelled after him. "And I should call the cops and have you arrested!"

My head was spinning. *Was my husband guilty? Would he have stolen from Larry, our employer, the man who co-signed the mortgage on our house and treated us like his children?*

"Did you know about this, Danielle?" Larry studied my face.

"No! Are you positive it was Jess?" I choked out.

"There is no doubt in my mind. He is guilty as sin. Danielle, I have to report him to the police."

"No! Please don't, Larry! How much money is missing? I'll work to pay it back!"

He wrote the amount down on paper and slid it toward me. It would take months to pay it back.

"I am begging you, Larry. You can deduct it from my check. Please don't call the cops! Jess will be thrown in jail! You'll get your money back. You have my word!"

Larry had hired us without a background check. At the time, he was desperate for help and thought Jess and I were a gift from above. He hired us on the spot, and we had made him proud for a long time… until now.

Was my husband a thief? Was there something in his past that he didn't reveal? I was hired at the saw blade company, but he was not. Did they do a background check on him and discover something? Jess was eager to leave Albuquerque. Something had happened with his employer. Was it something similar to this? His daughter was a thief; she stole constantly from me, and he blew it off as typical teenage behavior. Did the apple not fall far from the tree? Did I not know who my husband was?

Larry finally agreed to let me stay, work off Jess's debt, and not report the theft to the police. Larry had co-signed for our house; he would be left with the payments if we both left town. Larry liked me and treated me like a daughter. He had told me countless times that he had never known someone my age with my work ethic.

I returned home that evening to confront my husband. He was lying on the couch with a beer, three empty bottles on the floor beside him, and a cigarette dangling from his lips.

"Jess, did you take that money?" I studied his face.

"What if I did? Would you leave me?"

"Jess, did you take it?" I demanded an answer.

He left the couch and walked into the bathroom without another word, locking the door behind him.

I yelled through the door. "You need to get another job to help pay this debt to Larry! He said he won't call the cops if we pay him back!" He didn't answer. I pounded on the door. "Jess! Open this door! You need to explain why you took that money! You didn't need to do that! You've gone and ruined everything!"

"Leave me alone, Danielle! I don't need you, of all people, to judge me."

"What do you mean by that?!"

He didn't answer.

Jess searched for employment for several weeks but couldn't secure a job. He defaulted to cutting and bundling wood.

We attempted to continue with our lives, but the anxiety from the theft loomed over us like a dark cloud. We kept it from our friends, who were busy with their own lives, and I wanted them to view us in the same light.

While Jess and I were eating at a local hamburger stand one evening, we talked to a young woman holding her five-month-old baby on her lap. She mentioned needing to use the restroom and asked if I could watch her baby for a few minutes. Before I could respond, she placed the chubby baby in my arms and quickly headed toward the bathroom. I was entranced; it was the first time I had held a baby. The little boy peered into my eyes and beamed, and my heart softened. I bounced him and sang, "You are my sunshine," the only song I remembered from childhood. The mother returned shortly and thanked me.

Everything changed after Jess stole the money. When Larry came into the bowling alley, we only spoke business. He could no longer look me in the eye. He no longer asked me about my house projects, never asked what I did on my days off, and never mentioned Jess again. Our once close bond dissolved.

Our marriage changed. Jess seemed almost jealous that I was still working at the bowling alley. Some days, he didn't look for work and spent only an hour or two bundling wood.

I didn't know how to mend our marriage. For the past year, our life had been blissful. We had our own home, an active social life, and made more than enough money to live. But now, we didn't talk much and slept on separate sides of the bed. Jess's greed had destroyed everything we had built. After six long months, I had repaid all the money my husband had stolen.

I once looked at my husband with eyes full of love, but I couldn't do that any longer. Something inside me changed when I lost trust in the person I thought I could rely on. Unless I could turn back time, I knew things would always be different.

My intuition told me that my time at the bowling alley was over. I handed in my two-week resignation to Larry and had no idea what my next step would be.

"Jess," I said that evening. "I gave my notice at the bowling alley."

"Okay," he said with his nose buried in the newspaper.

"Jess, could you please put the paper down?"

He dropped the paper on the table and stared blankly at me.

"I called my mother, and she said I could stay with her for a few weeks. She's all alone now since my father died. Is that okay with you?"

"That's fine by me. Take the Hooptie. I've got my eye on a new pick-up truck."

I took a deep breath. I wanted to ask him where he would find the money to buy a new vehicle, but that would lead to an argument.

"I can't take the dog with me. My mother's landlady doesn't allow animals."

"I'm quite capable of taking care of the dog, Danielle. Jeez... Don't ya have any faith left in me?"

"Of course I do," I said convincingly, though I was lying. I had lost all faith in my husband, and I hoped that spending time away would help me find a new perspective.

TWENTY-FIVE

Madras

1988

MY MOTHER LEFT for work at six every morning and returned home after ten hours, typically cleaning two to three houses per day.

Jess always sounded cheerful whenever I called, and he said everything was going well. I avoided bringing up the subject of job hunting, as that put him in a sour mood. I decided to let him tell me when, or if, he found employment. Unfortunately, we had only enough money in the bank to cover next month's expenses, and neither of us was gainfully employed.

When my mother was at work, I had free time. I cleaned her apartment, went grocery shopping, and prepared dinner for her. I wanted to ease her burden while I was there.

While vacuuming, I found a file box in the corner of her closet. Curiosity got the best of me, so I took it out and set it on the bed. One by one, I pulled out each document and scanned it. For the most part, nothing was exciting or unusual, just receipts for items she had purchased. As I pulled out the last file and opened it, I discovered my birth certificate.

I was given the name Danielle King on the day I was born in Mitchell, South Dakota. It was hard to believe, and I had to laugh. My cousin Dottie confirmed that my father's legal name was Alouise A. Parise. *Where did the surname King come from? Why hadn't my mother shown me this document?* I took the document to my room and placed it in the lining of my suitcase. I might need it someday. Danielle King… It had a strange ring; I had never heard that version of my name before.

I hadn't heard from Jess in days and was starting to worry. I called him several times, but he didn't answer. I left message after message until, finally, my cell phone rang.

"Hi Jess, where have you been for the past week?"

"Working! I found a job!"

"That's wonderful news!" I said. "What kind of a job?"

"I'm cleaning offices in the evening."

"Oh," I tried to sound positive, but I was afraid my voice gave way to my disappointment. *A cleaning job… in an office where valuables are kept… the temptation may be too great.*

"It's not a great job, but the pay is decent."

"Well, I am happy. I imagine our bank account is dwindling."

"Ya, it certainly has, especially after I withdrew money to make a down payment on my new truck."

The money we had in the bank was reserved to pay our next mortgage. I held my tongue as Jess finally sounded happy, like his old self.

"How's our Danny? I miss him!"

"He's good. I'm sure he misses you, too."

"Say, Danielle, could you meet me for lunch tomorrow? We could meet in Redmond, which is halfway between us."

As a rule, I let Jess do all the driving. When I had to drive, I avoided highways. Driving in heavy traffic made my heart race, and I sometimes had to pull over and breathe into a paper bag. I didn't want to get behind the wheel again until I was heading back home to my husband.

"Why do you want to meet for lunch?" I said, puzzled. "I've been at my mother's for three weeks. It's time for me to come home."

I had forgiven Jess for what he did. He was not religious, nor did he have a spiritual bone in his body. It was up to me to lead him down the right path, and I felt confident I could help him become a better man. I was ready to go home and work on our marriage.

"Danielle…"

"What is it, Jess?"

"Never you mind. On second thought, I'll explain everything tomorrow."

TWENTY-SIX

Redmond

1988

I KNEW WHERE I was going... to a little restaurant Jess and I frequented when we first moved to Redmond. I left my mother's apartment at ten to avoid lunch-hour traffic. As I drove, I reflected on the past weeks...

I had always longed to spend quality time alone with my mother. During the weekends, we either went shopping or watched a movie together. She didn't behave like a widow consumed by grief.

Now in her mid-fifties, it seemed my mother had forgotten many aspects of her life, including her extended family—at least, that was my impression. Twenty years ago, after Christmas Day in Ottawa, she had no further contact with her family.

I have always wondered how her family found us on Christmas Day in 1967. One evening, I got up the courage to ask...

"Ma, how do you think your family found on Christmas Day when we lived in Ottawa? Did they hire a private investigator?"

"Hmmm… Maybe someone wrote them a letter," she said with a wink.

Taking that step must have required great courage from her. My father would never have permitted it, and she faced the risk of his rage had he discovered she wrote a letter to her family.

That evening, I told her that we should contact her family.

"They won't even remember me, Danielle. It's been too many years."

"Ma, you're wrong!"

I searched the *White Pages* for her relatives, but none lived in Oregon. My mother was at work, and I knew she would disapprove of what I was about to do. I called the Canadian information operator.

"Do you have the phone number of anyone living in Hornepayne with the last name Gauchier?" I was desperate. I would call anyone in the family to break my mother's isolation from her family.

The operator replied, *"I have Camille Gauchier's phone number. Do you want that one?"*

I couldn't believe my luck. My Uncle Camille was still living in Hornepayne. I dialed as fast as my fingers could move.

"Hello?" a woman's voice answered.

"Hi, you don't know me, but…"

"Oh my God, Theresa!" the woman screamed.

"No, this is Theresa's daughter, Danielle! Aunt Adrianne?" I asked, but she didn't hear me. She was already calling my uncle to the phone.

"Danielle?! Is it really you?!"

"Yes, this is Danielle, Uncle Camille!" It felt amazing to say his name again. He asked how and where I was. He asked where my sister was. I heard a commotion in the background. My aunt had gone next door to tell more of the relatives that I was on the phone. Before I knew it, the phone was passed from relative to relative, and I was talking with aunts and uncles I hadn't seen since childhood. They had many questions and were unaware that my father had died.

When my mother returned from work, I told her I had contacted her family. Her face went white.

"Ma, they were so happy to talk to me! You should call them right now! Uncle Camille gave me Grandmother's phone number." I gave her the number on scrap paper and felt as if I was passing her the most precious thing in all the world.

"You shouldn't have done that, Danielle! I can't talk to them!" She left the room.

Then it dawned on me... She would have to account for the past twenty years. She would need to explain why she never contacted her family, why we disappeared without a trace, and why her daughters did not receive an education. The weight of responsibility on her shoulders was overwhelming.

I arrived at the restaurant an hour early. I parked, turned the radio on to a rock station, and rested my head against the seat. Relaxation was unfamiliar to me. Being unemployed was also unfamiliar. I had worked my entire life. *Whatever Jess has to say, we will work through it. We can sell the house, move to a new city, recreate ourselves, and start fresh.* I had done that many times before. I loved our run-down house but could easily walk away from it. It held terrible memories. It was the house where I discovered that my husband was a thief.

I had dozed off and was awakened by a soft tap on the window. It was Jess. He smiled and waved at me through the glass, and my heart filled with joy at the sight of him.

He requested to sit in the restaurant's corner booth and asked the waitress to bring us coffee.

"I missed you! We've never spent much time apart before," I exclaimed as the waitress poured our coffee. I couldn't stop smiling; Jess smiled sheepishly back.

"Yeah, a lot can happen in a few weeks," he nodded and thanked the waitress. "I know ya weren't happy with me when ya left."

"I wasn't, but we can work through this... I know that now. I've done a lot of thinking, and I have an idea... We can sell the house and move. We could move to Madras so I could be close to my mother. We could change our last name and get a fresh new start!"

Jess jerked his head back as if he had been hit with a bat.

"Danielle, Listen to yourself!"

I was embarrassed. *Why did I say that?* There had to be another way—a normal way—to work through this. I was desperate to make our marriage work, so desperate that I fell back on old habits. What would ordinary people do in this situation? My history taught me to deal with a problem in only one way... run.

We silently studied the menu for a few minutes when the waitress approached. We both ordered a club sandwich.

"I'm not very hungry," I said after we placed our order.

"Neither am I." Jess lit a cigarette. I reached across the table and took a puff. I had not had a cigarette since I went to my mother's; the smoke calmed my nerves.

The conversation turned to our dog, Danny. Jess had taken him on a camping trip in my absence, and the dog discovered that he loved to jump into the lake after the fish. Our laughter lightened the mood, and I wanted to stay in that happy moment forever.

But the fact was that my husband stole from our employer, who was also our friend. Would I ever trust him again or pretend it never happened? I was leaning toward the latter.

He explained his new job and said he had to clean up after the "pigs in the office." I shook my head in disgust as I agreed with every word he said.

The waitress cleared our table and gave us the tab. Jess pulled out his wallet and began counting the bills.

"I'll pay half," I offered.

"I've got this," he said firmly.

"At least let me pay the tip," I offered again.

"Danielle, please stop."

His voice sounded stern as if he were angry with me. I thought perhaps he wasn't over the fact I had abruptly left to stay with my mother.

"Danielle… I asked ya here for a reason…"

"What is it, Jess? I thought you missed me and were going to tell me to come home," I said with hope. "I have my suitcase in the car."

"Danielle, I can't get the image of ya holding that baby out of my mind. Your face lit up in a way I had never seen before. I can't deny ya that."

"I don't want a baby! We have Danny, and we have each other!"

"Danielle, there is something else…"

My heart stood still. *What else could he possibly say?*

"I've fallen in love with someone else," he said, looking off to the side of the room, avoiding eye contact.

"What! Who have you fallen in love with?!" I demanded.

"Her name is Linda."

"Linda? You don't mean the older woman who works at the snack bar at the bowling alley?" I snickered.

"Yes, and she's *my* age, Danielle."

"She's my mother's age!" I said in disgust.

People were starting to look our way, so we walked outside to the parking lot to continue the conversation. Jess leaned against the building and lit a cigarette.

"Danielle, ya can't tell me that our age difference has not caused problems in our marriage," he said calmly.

"Our age difference has never been a problem for me. Your being a thief is what caused problems in our marriage! Don't blame this on the fact that you think I need a child or the difference in our ages! I was gone for only three weeks, and you had an affair!" I nearly screamed. "The problems in this marriage are one hundred percent your fault!"

"I'll file for divorce at the courthouse... And if it's okay with you, I'd like to keep the house." He had his plan laid out before he entered the restaurant, and I had been gazing at him starry-eyed, waiting for him to tell me that he missed me and it was time to come home.

"What should I do next?!" I half-cried. It was all too much. Within a few minutes, I discovered that my husband was cheating on me; I was single again, and I was homeless.

I fought back tears. I would not let him see me cry. I had to be strong—I had been through far worse.

"What about Danny?" I asked.

"Do ya want to share custody of the dog?" he sounded surprised.

I had previously parted ways with dogs and lived through the sadness. Danny could not be alone all day in my mother's apartment while I worked. He barked incessantly, and the neighbors would complain.

"On second thought, I think Danny should stay with you," I said. "I'll drive down next week to collect my things. Feel free to pack my stuff up."

"Danielle..."

"What?" I said, irritation in my voice.

"Thank you for understanding."

"I don't understand!" Yelling loudly, I cried out. "What did I do wrong? Was I a good wife?" I studied his face for an answer. I had given him my best. I cooked our meals, kept the house clean, did the laundry, fed the dog, and took on house projects without his assistance.

"Yes, Danielle, you were a wonderful wife," he said softly to calm me.

"Well, life goes on then, doesn't it?" I said bravely, then turned and walked toward my car.

Another man had let me down. What did I expect? I had lived alone before I met Jess, and I was happy. I would figure life out again... I'd reinvent myself. Now that my father was out of the picture, I believed my mother would let me live with her for as long as needed. I would find a job, save every penny, and decide my next move.

TWENTY-SEVEN

Madras

1988-89

I BECAME ACQUAINTED with a lady who lived in my mother's apartment building. After she heard that I was going through a divorce, she offered me a job as a waitress at the restaurant she managed.

Two weeks later, I returned to my house in Bend, now Jess's house, to pack up my belongings and give my dog Danny hugs and kisses. I was pleasantly surprised that Jess had packed my things, but it made sense since he needed the room for Linda, who was in the process of moving in.

After loading the boxes into my car, Jess and I went to the courthouse to have my name removed from the house deed. We had built some equity in our home, but he told me to keep the Hooptie, and we called it even.

I was sure that without my paycheck, he would need help to make ends meet. Even though it was no longer my business, I asked him how he would find the money for the house payment.

"I receive my unemployment check, and Linda pays half of the bills," he answered. I searched his face. Was he embarrassed by his lack of motivation? I saw only the same expression I had seen for the past three years, and I wondered whether his lack of ambition concerned his new girlfriend.

My anger toward Jess was waning, and I was oddly grateful that someone cared for him. Strangely, I still wanted Jess in my life in some capacity, and I sensed he wanted me in his.

"Maybe I can come down sometime when Linda is here, and you can throw a steak on the grill," I said in a friendly manner.

"Let's do that!" Jess said enthusiastically. "I'm sure Linda would like to visit with you, too!"

Our divorce was simple… We argued over nothing and walked away with what we came into the marriage with—the clothes on our backs.

My mother finally gathered the courage to call her mother. I wasn't home when she made the call, so I didn't hear how she explained the missing years away.

Following the initial phone call, my mother wept for days. My grandmother revealed that her younger sister, Noelle, and her son, Jon, had perished in a car accident in 1971. They had been dead for seventeen years, and my mother was completely unaware. I thought my heart would break for my cousins, Terri and Michelle. As teenagers, they lost both their little brother and their mother.

The phone rang frequently after Ma called her mother, connecting with one long-lost sibling or another. She conversed with them in her native

French, so I only caught fragments of their conversations.

During a conversation one evening with one of her younger brothers, I heard my mother say, "Je n'ai jamais vécu à Athabasca," which translates to, "I never lived in Athabasca." When their conversation ended, I questioned her.

"Ma, we lived in Athabasca for two years! Why did you lie to your brother?"

"Someone tracked us down. Oil was discovered on the property, and someone wanted to purchase it."

"Oil! Are we rich?!" I exclaimed.

"No... And do *not* mention this to your sister."

"Didn't Daddy sell the farm in Athabasca?" I remembered him taking the horses to auction and giving away our dogs, but I had no idea how my parents managed their finances.

"No, he did *not* sell the farm. We left it," she said, as if abandoning property were perfectly normal.

"We have to call them! Ma! We could be rich!"

"Danielle!" she said sternly. "I said, ignore this! I should have never told you!"

"Ma, why don't you want the money?" I was just as confused as I had been while growing up. Nothing ever made sense—all the running, all the hiding. Now that my father was dead, I thought I would finally figure things out.

"Danielle... This is not your concern."

It was as if my father was sitting in the corner of the room, puffing away on a cigarette. My mother was still afraid of him.

One evening, while my mother and I were washing the dinner dishes, she had a question.

"My older brother Peter... We were very close growing up..." She paused as she searched for the words to explain the situation. "Aunt Ann said that he did something to his daughters... He was arrested and thrown in jail."

My heart started to race. *Is she going to ask me about my father? Is she about to admit she knows what he did?*

"Danielle... Do you think he was molesting his daughters?" she said in a curious tone.

Why is she asking me this? She had the conversation with Aunt Ann, not me. Has she already formed an opinion and now wants to hear mine? Why would my opinion matter?

She studied my face as she waited for me to answer. If I answered "yes," she might ask further questions. My answer could change everything... our relationship and life as we knew it.

"No, I don't think Uncle Peter would do that to his daughters."

She flashed a smile. Either she was innocent and knew nothing of my father's actions, or I had just absolved her of guilt.

"Aunt Ann also said that your grandmother used to sit by the window every day and pray the rosary for our return. She never gave up on us..." Her voice cracked.

"Oh, Ma!" I dropped my dish towel and wrapped my arms around her. Her shoulders trembled as she attempted to hold back her tears. She pulled away from me and dried her eyes.

"Danielle, I'm going home... to Hornepayne."

"What? Ma, no!" I cried.

"I will give the landlord thirty days' notice next week when I pay the rent. You can stay here for the next month; then, you'll have to find a more affordable apartment."

"Ma, I'll go with you!"

"No, Danielle. I have to do this alone," she said with finality. "I'll come back someday... after your grandmother passes." I didn't believe her.

Why couldn't I go with her? Did she want time to catch up with her family without her divorced daughter tagging along? Her family remained strict Catholics. Was she afraid they would pass judgment on me? Or did she just need to create distance between herself and her daughters?

As she packed the boxes, she looked older than her fifty-seven years. She had worked hard all her life, taking any employment she could find. She had worked at state fairs, sold jewelry in Nashville, worked at lunch counters, and taken in sewing. It was no wonder that her shoulders were slumped.

Two of my uncles arrived several days later and packed all her boxes into a truck. I wanted to crawl into a crack in the earth and never come out. My mother was leaving.

She gave me her Ford Escort before she left. The Hooptie had become undrivable, and I never did have the rear window replaced. After a month passed, I moved out of my mother's apartment and into a smaller efficiency in the same complex.

One evening, there was a knock at my door. It was Jess. He was holding a suitcase.

He flopped on the couch. The reason for his visit was a mystery. He looked confused.

"Jess, what are you doing here?"

"I want ya back. I made a mistake."

"What about Linda? I thought you loved her?" I said with a hint of sarcasm.

He stayed for two days, begging me to return to him the entire time. But too much had happened between us, and I stood firm in my decision to move on with my life. When he said he couldn't return to Linda, I told him it was time to leave; his relationship with Linda was not my problem.

Since my mother left for Ottawa, I pinched every penny and donated most of my belongings to charity. I sold the Escort, stuffed my clothes into a suitcase, and bought a one-way bus ticket to Moriarty. I had 1,300 miles ahead of me.

I could have remained in Madras, but my heart wanted to return to my sister; we had unfinished business. Karole remained the stoic sister as an adult, while I was too softhearted—remnants of our childhood. Maybe together, I could become stronger, and Karole's heart would soften. I saw Karole only once during the time I lived in Oregon. We talked on the phone occasionally, but long distance was expensive, and our conversations were brief. We had lost our once-shared closeness, and I wanted it back.

As the bus left Oregon, I knew I would miss the evergreen woods, the Cascade Mountain range, and the high, rolling, wind-swept plains. I would miss camping near the rivers and lakes. And I would miss Jess.

From the beginning, our marriage faced challenges. The age difference was notable, but a much greater divide existed in our ambitions. Jess preferred the path of least resistance, which ultimately led to our downfall. It wasn't about him falling for another woman; Linda was merely a symptom of the deeper problems in our relationship.

Karole and Phil picked me up at the bus station in Moriarty. I was impressed as we drove up to their mobile home, surrounded by acres of land. Karole proudly gave me a tour and showed me the guest bedroom, which she said was mine for as long as I wanted. A few days later, Phil pulled a few strings and got me a full-time job in the shoe department at Montgomery Ward.

TWENTY-EIGHT

Moriarty

1989

AFTER MY FATHER'S passing, my cousin Dottie and I had several phone conversations, but the frequency of our calls diminished as life got busy. One day at work, I saw that I had missed a call from her. She left a message asking me to return her call as soon as possible. I couldn't help but wonder if Aunt Gladys had passed away.

Once Karole and I finished washing the dishes, I returned to my room and closed the door. I called Dottie.

"Dottie, hi! Is everything okay? Is Aunt Gladys all right?"

"Yes, Gladys is fine. She's slowing down a bit, but she's fine."

"What's up?" I said cheerfully, glad to hear her voice again.

"Danielle... Are you sitting down?"

"I'm lying on my bed. Nothing you could say would make me fall over," I said with a half-laugh.

"Don't be too sure of that... I have a lot to tell you, and I'm not sure where to begin."

"Start at the beginning, Dottie." Judging by the tone of her voice, something was wrong.

"Do you remember I told you that my daughter's fiancé, Scott, works for a branch of the CIA?"

"Yes, and I told you not to bother him to investigate my father's past."

"Well, Scott and my daughter married last spring, and I *did* bother him, Danielle. I did it not only for you but for Aunt Gladys. She had always wondered what happened to her brother. She said Jack was a troubled kid who ran away from home at an early age. Scott found out things about your father—bad things. If you don't want to hear it, stop me from going further. But the information I have might explain a lot about your childhood."

Did I want to know? Karole and I were in a good place in our lives. We had confessed our deepest, darkest secrets that we kept locked away from each other. Karole and Phil had a lovely marriage, home, and a decent life. I felt loved and blessed to have a place to stay while building a new life after my divorce. Did I want to upset all of that?

There was a pause in our conversation as I weighed the pros and cons. My mind spun back to the confusion of my childhood. At this time, my life was under control and even pleasant. I had finally found normalcy... and now this...

"Danielle?" Dottie thought our phones had disconnected.

"I'm here. What did you find out?" My lips spoke involuntarily—my brain had not yet decided what I wanted to do.

"Your father served in the U.S. Army in his early twenties under the name Alouise A. Parise. From what Scott could tell, that was probably one of the only times he used his legal name. He was married during that time."

"He told me he was in a 'short-lived marriage' before marrying my mother."

"He was married *three* times, Danielle… His short-lived marriage was his first and produced no children. He married for a second time when he enlisted in the Canadian Army. After the war, he, his wife, and their daughter relocated to Spokane, and they had a second daughter. His marriage to your mother was his third."

"I have two half-sisters?"

"Yes, Danielle, their names are Jeannie and Janet."

"If my mother was aware of this, she never told me."

This was a lot to take in. My father had a whole life before he met and married my mother. Her Catholic faith would have prevented her from marrying him if she had known he was divorced.

"There's more, Danielle—a lot more. Damn, I wish we were face-to-face," Dottie said sadly. "This is not the kind of news that should be given over the phone."

"It's okay. Go on," I encouraged.

"There is no way to soften what I'm about to tell you…"

"Just say it, Dottie." I felt my heart beating in my throat. *How much worse can this conversation get?*

"Danielle, your father raped his daughter, Jeannie, when she was a little girl."

"Oh, my God!" It wasn't only Karole and me. We weren't the first.

"There's more, Danielle... his brother-in-law, Ralph, walked into the room and caught him in the act.... Danielle? Are you still there?"

"I'm here." I was in a state of shock, and there was a high-pitched ringing in my ears. How much more could I endure? I was thrown down a rabbit hole, and there was nothing to grab hold of to slow the descent. Dottie continued.

"Your father then beat his brother-in-law to a bloody pulp and left him for dead. Ralph spent weeks in the hospital and underwent multiple surgeries."

"Is Ralph okay?" I asked.

"He survived, but he was never the same again."

I wanted to be sick. All this time, I thought it was only my sister and me he had damaged. He had caused devastation to another entire family. Other children had suffered, and he forever changed another man's life.

"The police went to find your father the day after the incident, but he had disappeared. He abandoned his wife and two children and went into hiding. He was wanted for rape and attempted murder charges. I'm sure your father thought he killed Ralph, and that may be why your family was constantly on the move. Your father always managed to stay one step ahead of the law."

"How is Jeannie? Is she okay?" My heart ached for my half-sister.

"Jeannie is married now and has a family. I have no idea what her mental state is."

A memory crashed into my mind... a visit to a young woman named Jeannie, a "friend" of my father's. She held a baby on her hip and had a toddler's hand in the other. My parents spoke to her at her front doorway for a few minutes, and then we left abruptly. My father shouted, "She's rude!" as he walked back to our car, loud enough for Jeannie to hear.

"Dottie... I think I met her," I stated flatly.

"You met who?"

"I met Jeannie... years ago... in the early 70s."

"How did that come about?"

"We drove to her house. I had no idea what was said. She and my parents talked briefly. Then we left."

"Wow, your father had balls going to visit the very daughter he raped. Did he think Jeannie would welcome him back with open arms?"

"Where are my half-sisters now?"

"I'll ask Scott if he has their addresses. Do you want to meet them?" Dottie said, surprised by my curiosity.

"I don't know if I do or not. At the very least, I'd like to know they are okay."

"With a sick fuck for a father, how could they be," Dottie said sarcastically. "Jeannie and Janet would be ten or more years older than you. You have nieces and nephews you've never met." Dottie hesitated before asking the next thing on her mind. "Danielle... did he do to you what he did to your half-sister?"

"No!" I exclaimed as if it were the silliest question in the world. "He was a good father!"

On top of everything I had just learned, a confession was something I wasn't ready to give. I would cover for him, as I'd done forever. I would continue to protect him, even though I had just found out that he was an incestuous serial rapist.

"Aunt Gladys collected articles about your father throughout the years. Some were from his early years as a professional boxer and wrestler. When he returned from the war, he wrote several articles for a local newspaper about his experiences during the war. Would you like me to mail them to you?"

"Yes, please," I answered, unsure why I would want to read about the man who tried to ruin my life.

"Some of the articles are pretty crude and describe what it was like to fight in the war. And I'll warn you... it's confusing to read the articles... he used several surnames."

"I lost track of how many surnames he—or should I say, 'we'—used."

"After I read the articles, I surmised that your father was a hot-tempered, heavy-drinking soldier with a sharp tongue and a quick temper who always had the last word in an argument. His temper caused him to be promoted and demoted more than once."

"I'm not surprised," I sighed. "All my life, I thought he was angry at me, but apparently, his anger existed long before I was born."

After our conversation ended, I stared at my bedroom door. Karole was in the living room with her husband. I heard the television and occasional laughter; they must be watching something funny. But I had to tell her.

It's unclear when my mother discovered my father's first family, but he shared this information with her at some point. She never informed my sister and me about our two half-sisters. Did she know about his ex-wife and two daughters before marrying him? Was she aware of the reasons for our constant moves, or did she follow my father's instructions blindly?

I thought I would be free of him after his death. I had been trying so hard to forget everything that had happened. Hadn't I suffered enough? What right did he have to upset my life now? I hoped the worms found him and made him suffer for what he did to us… and to his other daughters. When would the pain and confusion he caused end? I felt the all-too-familiar twist in my stomach.

"Karole, let's go for a walk…"

TWENTY-NINE

Moriarty

1989

KAROLE WAS ALWAYS the strong sister—the girl who could be lifted off her feet by her ponytail and show no fear. But as she listened to me tell the news from our cousin, her face cringed at the details.

We were exploring unknown territory... Our father had harmed others before us; we weren't the first. Karole fought to conceal her feelings and uphold her usual courageous demeanor, but her eyes grew wide as she absorbed the details as they were revealed.

There is always someone who has it worse than you. Karole had it worse than I did. At least I had fifteen years before the absolute insanity started. She didn't have that luxury, and it was anyone's guess how long she'd been suffering at his hands. I don't think she even knew.

Believing she needed the information, I considered how I delivered it. I could have chosen gentler words, but it was too late. I had already uttered every harsh syllable.

"I hope he is burning in the fires of hell! I hope the devil is poking him with pitchforks!" Karole screamed. She couldn't catch her breath. I had never seen her so upset.

Our father had raped our step-sister. His brother-in-law caught him in the act, then was beaten and left for dead. He abandoned his wife and two young daughters. He recreated himself and even fooled our mother into thinking he was someone he was not. Then, he had two more daughters. And the cycle of abuse continued.

"He thought he had killed his brother-in-law. That poor man was only trying to stop him, and our father beat him to a pulp. Daddy was a professional boxer. Can you even imagine how strong he was?"

"Stop it, Danielle!"

"Stop what?" I had no idea what she meant.

"Stop calling him Daddy!" Karole scolded. "Daddy is an endearing name, and he doesn't deserve it! I never want to hear you call him that again!"

I felt childish. Calling my father "Daddy" was a habit from childhood.

"What should I call him then?" I asked.

"Anything but Daddy! Call him The Asshole, The Pervert... Call him The Sick, Twisted Fuck! Get creative, Danielle!"

It seemed as if Karole's very soul had ignited. She and I harbored different levels of anger toward my father. Karole would have attacked if he had been standing before us.

Every so often, her deeply rooted issues caused her to criticize those around her, so I bore the brunt of her harsh words now and then. I knew her outbursts were not directed at me; she needed to vent. Despite her emotional meltdowns, she would revert to her courageous and determined self, but I always sensed that another breakdown was on the horizon.

I felt a blend of bitterness and sympathy. As a child, he must have experienced pain. Something in his upbringing had faltered. He never grasped how to be loving or caring; a crucial part of his personality was absent. He once confided that he had suffered abuse as a child. Could that explain his cruelty towards us?

"I believe he couldn't change his nature," I said, attempting to understand our father's behavior. "He experienced a terrible childhood."

"Many people experience terrible childhoods!" Karole exclaimed sharply. "Why would making a child suffer help someone feel better about themselves? Your argument doesn't hold up, Danielle. You're the Bible thumper. Doesn't God grant all of us 'free will'? Our father used his free will to make people suffer. He knew what he did was wrong... That's why he ran!"

Karole was on the verge of exploding. I chose to stop analyzing and making excuses for our father. She had her own unique experiences with him and deserved to express herself however she felt needed. If pushed, her temper could fly from zero to one hundred in a blink. She ignored most of life's irritants and seemed unfazed by negative things that happened to her, but when she reached the end of her rope, all hell could break loose.

How did our father influence our identities? What could my sister and I have accomplished if given different chances? My sister projected an image of a tough cookie, leading others to believe nothing could upset her. In contrast, I was more timid. Yet, we shared one commonality... We both constantly lived in fear. The fear lingered into adulthood. Karole's bravado and my gentle shyness acted as our shield against the anxiety that awaited us at every turn.

"I wish the authorities had found him before he met Ma. I wish someone had tossed his sorry ass in prison and thrown away the key," Karole said succinctly.

"Then you and I wouldn't be here," I said gently. "Then we wouldn't be sisters."

"Oh, Danielle, we *never* should have been born!"

We walked for several minutes, gazing at the road ahead. The information from Cousin Dottie was overwhelming.

Karole broke the silence. "Where do we go from here? What do we do with this information?"

"What are our choices?" I asked.

"We can do what we've always done... nothing," Karole said. "We can stuff the information deep in our guts with all the other shit and never discuss it again."

"I would like to find our half-sisters!" I said with the enthusiasm of a child. "Then we could apologize to them."

"Danielle... We have nothing to apologize for! They wouldn't want to meet us. Think about it... We are half 'him,' and we'd remind them of their past. A visit from us would reopen old wounds."

"Should we take this information to the police?" I innocently asked.

"I'm sure Dottie's son-in-law has already passed this information to the authorities. Our father has passed away, so there's no one to prosecute. Ma is in Canada, and they certainly aren't going to pursue her; the crime occurred years before he met her."

"Maybe if we find Jeannie and Janet, we could support each other," I said softly, half-expecting my sister to shoot down the idea.

"That would happen only in a perfect world, sister. They would slam the door in our faces."

"But they are our family!" I continued to protest. "We have nieces and nephews we haven't met!"

"Danielle, forget it. We are never going to contact them. And if you do, don't tell me. I don't want to be part of it. Do you really want to meet Ralph? He's probably brain-damaged and drooling in a wheelchair. Meeting those people would cause more drama than I need. Jeannie and Janet may be our relatives, but that doesn't mean a thing to me. They are related to us by blood, his blood, and his blood is bad blood!"

"Should we tell Phil?" I asked sheepishly, already knowing the answer.

"He doesn't need to know any of this!"

After entering the house, we made our way to the kitchen. Karole appeared cool, calm, and collected—Phil would never have guessed she had just learned information that rocked her world. Karole opened the refrigerator and searched around.

"Are you hungry already? We just finished dinner an hour ago," I asked.

"Where are the leftover mashed potatoes?" She found the bowl, grabbed a fork, and sat at the table.

"You're going to eat that cold?" I asked. "Let me heat it for you."

"It's fine." She stared straight ahead as she ate. "Danielle, let's call Ma… and tell her what Dottie told you."

"Karole, no! We can never tell Ma!"

"Why the hell not? The news might not surprise her; she probably already knows. I want to ask her if this was the reason she and the asshole dragged us all over the continent. Were our father's sins the reason we couldn't go to school? And I'd like to ask her the big question... Did she know what he was doing to us? Danielle, doesn't all this make you spitting mad?!"

"Yes, it makes me mad! But we are okay now... He's dead, and we're making our way in the world. Ma got us lots of books to read, and..."

"Stop making excuses for her, Danielle!" Karole said in a low whisper so her husband wouldn't overhear in the next room.

"Karole, I am bitter, too, but I'm trying to get on with life by not adding unnecessary drama. Telling Ma would create the ultimate drama. She'd never speak to us again! She's all we have left."

"You mean, she's all *you* have left. She doesn't care about me. She never did." Karole said flatly.

"That's not true! She loves you, too!" I protested, knowing there was some truth to it. "If you told Ma, you'd get a few moments of revenge, but would that make you happy? Inflicting our pain onto her is what our father did to us, and he was never a happy man."

Karole was wearing me down. So many times in the past, she threatened to tell our mother about the abuse, and every time, I stopped her.

I grabbed a spoon and began to share the bowl of cold potatoes with Karole.

"I can't help but wonder what she knew about him," Karole said thoughtfully. "I think when they married, she knew nothing. But he must have told her something along the way. I'm sure he made up some bullshit reason for running from the law, and I'm sure he was the victim in his version of the story. Whenever he announced that we were moving again, I saw pain in her eyes, but she never argued with him. She dutifully packed up. She must have known he was running from someone or something. And whatever bullshit story he fed her, she believed it."

"She couldn't have known his entire history," I explained. "She would have left him! If she knew he raped his daughter from a previous marriage, common sense would have told her that he would do it to *her* daughters, too. Ma had *no* idea who she married, and I believe she didn't see the change in my personality after he raped me or that my clothes were dirty and my hair was full of leaves."

"I saw the change in you the moment you came out of the woods that day. Why wouldn't your own mother notice? Believe what you want, Danielle. She took her marriage vows, 'For better or for worse,' and her religious beliefs would *never* have allowed her to leave him. Don't you think a woman notices when her husband constantly isolates her child?"

"He told me that Ma didn't like sex," I added as another excuse for what he did to us.

"He told me the same thing. That is not something a father should tell his daughter!" Karole scolded. "I, too, want to believe that Ma had no inkling why he took me on 'business trips' and then showered me with gifts, and when I got my period, he left me home and began taking you. I knew exactly what was happening when you returned home with gifts. I want to believe that Ma never put two and two together… but Danielle, I can't."

"Do you want Ma to spend her remaining years crying for us? Because if you tell her, that's what will happen. She's finally in a good place, Karole."

"She wouldn't cry for us! She's all but written us out of her life! We're a reminder of her past!" Karole almost laughed.

"Karole! She will die if you tell her!"

I didn't know how to appeal to my sister's heart. How could I make her feel love for our mother when she never had a loving relationship with her in the first place? How could I stop her from making my mother's world implode? My mother was back in the heart of her family and sounded happy when we talked. She had so little happiness in her marriage. She deserved to be happy again.

"Once Ma married, her life was filled with turmoil, and the truth is, we don't know what she understood about him. She might have been that naive. My relationship with her was different from yours. If you tell Ma what we found out about our father—her husband—I will lose her forever. Karole, can you do this for me? Can we keep this between us?"

She set down her fork and rubbed her eyes while searching for an answer. "I'll do it for you… but if I explode someday from keeping all this shit locked inside, that's on you!"

Karole had been my lifelong protector. She always kept an eye on me while we were growing up and continued to do so. Her promises were as good as gold. We would not tell my mother, and she could live out the rest of her life in peace.

I jumped up and threw my arms around her.

"You know I love you."

"You'd better love me!" Karole half-laughed.

I did love her. I doubted that two sisters could be closer. We shared a bond that no one else could understand.

"Karole, have you ever thought about having a baby?" I asked her one warm evening as we shared a cigarette at the picnic table in front of her trailer.

"It's crossed my mind. If Phil had his way, we'd have four kids by now."

"If I had a kid, I would raise him or her differently than we were raised," I said definitively.

"Well, I would hope so!" Karole laughed sarcastically.

I had often dreamed of the type of parent I'd be. I would buy a lovely home where my child could grow up and attend school. He or she would have lots of friends. I would help my child every evening with their homework, and at bedtime, I'd tuck him into bed on a soft mattress with fresh sheets. I would tell my child that I loved him and shield him from the evil in the world. But I didn't have a man, so it was a dream.

"I don't know how I feel about having a kid. I don't know what kind of mother I'd be," Karole sighed.

"Be the kind of mother that Ma was!"

"Are you kidding me?" She looked at me as if I had three eyes.

"I mean, be the kind of mother Ma *wanted* to be."

"Why wasn't Ma the kind of mother she wanted to be in the first place? I don't buy it, Danielle. Your undying devotion to her will always remain a mystery to me."

I would always disagree with Karole's opinion of our mother. To me, she was loving and did her best to improve my life. To Karole, she was a woman who seemed resentful toward her for reasons she could never understand. We were two sisters from the same family, but our experiences drastically differed.

Perhaps it was for the best that neither of us had children. Our emotional scars likely would have affected our ability to be good parents. At that time, I found it difficult enough to care for myself.

A large manila envelope from my cousin Dottie arrived in the mail. I sat at the kitchen table and tore it open. On top of the stack was a photo of my father as a young man. He posed for the camera bare-chested and held his fist clenched as if ready to punch. I placed it face down. I scanned the articles he had written for a local newspaper after the war. He described how he enlisted without telling his wife or saying goodbye to her or his daughter. The article included a picture of him with his then-wife and young daughter, Jeannie. Not long after the picture was taken, the incident occurred, and he disappeared from their lives without any explanation, never to return. I stared at the photo of little Jeannie and prayed that she had no memory of what he had done to her.

In one of the articles, he wrote…

"I didn't know whether I wanted to see my wife or not after returning home from the war, as she was still pretty mad about me going away as I did."

My heart ached for his then-wife. He wasn't running from the law yet, but he was already hurting people in other ways.

I tucked the articles back and slid the envelope into the bottom of my sweater drawer. Maybe I'd read them another day.

*My father's first family
(daughter Jeannie on his lap)*

THIRTY

Albuquerque

1989-90

"I'M GOING TO look for an apartment," I said to Karole as we washed the dishes one evening. "I saved money when I stayed with Ma, and I saved nearly everything I've earned at Montgomery Ward since moving in with you."

"You don't have to leave," Karole said sadly.

"It's time," I said fearlessly. "You two lovebirds need your privacy."

"Don't go disappearing again like you did when you moved to Oregon," Karole reprimanded.

"I promise I'll find an apartment close by."

I became acquainted with Vicky, who worked behind the snack bar at Montgomery Ward. She was looking for a roommate to split the rent. The location of her apartment was in Albuquerque near Coronado Mall, and paying half the rent was all I could afford on my salary. Finding a better-paying job was first on my to-do list.

Vicky's apartment was tidy, and the furniture was understated yet pleasant. We shook hands to seal the deal, and I moved in the following day.

Vicky and I became fast friends. Living with her was easy, and it may have been the most stress-free place I had ever lived. There was no father to contend with, no husband lazing on the couch with a beer and a cigarette, and no guilt about intruding on someone's privacy. We enjoyed each other's company. On our days off, we went to the movie theater or bowling. Sometimes, we'd rent a video and pop a giant bowl of popcorn. Vicky had an occasional date, but her interest in men waned after two or three dates. I thought she was too picky about men, but she said she had high standards and didn't want to repeat her past mistakes.

I wasn't interested in dating at that time. It felt refreshing to have only myself to answer to. My mother's advice, "Stay single if possible," had become more meaningful than ever.

Karole was determined to start her own business and opened a T-shirt shop in the mall. Like my father, she claimed that she could sell anything to anyone. She had been prescient and kept her job at the optical store, giving her that to fall back on when the rent at the mall became too expensive, forcing her to close the T-shirt store.

I applied for a job as a cashier at Sandia Bowl. The hourly pay was twice what I made at Montgomery Ward. During the interview, I told the manager about my extensive experience working in bowling alleys. He raised his eyebrows; he realized I could efficiently run the place with one arm tied behind my back. I was relieved he didn't ask for references; my last employment at a bowling alley had ended badly. Larry, my former employer, might give me a glowing reference, but I didn't want to take the chance that he would mention I was married to a thief. For all Larry knew, I was still married to Jess.

I was hired shortly after the interview and was thrilled to see the salary increase. After paying the bills, I had money left over and could start saving again instead of living paycheck to paycheck. After several weeks, I became acquainted with Lee, who was the supervisor of the pro shop. Lee told me his marriage was "on the rocks." We began hanging out after work, and he couldn't stop complaining about his wife.

Karole started missing work, which was unusual for her. In recent months, Karole experienced abdominal and back pain and often wanted to remain in bed all day.

One evening, as I watched the news from the couch, my phone rang. It was Phil, and he sounded frantic.

"I had to call an ambulance! She passed out! They did a bunch of tests at the hospital, and an ultrasound showed something on her ovaries. They think she might have cancer. They are waiting for her blood tests to come back. She's scheduled for a hysterectomy in the morning."

My thoughts started to swirl... Nothing could hurt Karole. The doctors had to be wrong.

"I'll call in sick to work tomorrow and meet you at the hospital." I had no words of comfort to offer. I needed words of comfort myself.

I hung up the phone and dialed my mother. Since she moved to Hornepayne, I called her every Sunday afternoon. She held two jobs: her day job was waitressing at a cafe, and her evening job was washing dishes at a restaurant. Any free time she found was filled with activities with her family. She sounded content, or at least as content as my mother could be, and whenever I phoned her, I felt as if I was intruding. I told myself she had missed so much with her family over the years and was making up for lost time.

"Ma, Karole is in the hospital!" I blurted out.

"What's wrong with her?"

"I'm not sure. She passed out at home, and Phil called an ambulance. The doctors did an ultrasound and saw something on her ovaries. They think she might have ovarian cancer!" I heard my mother gasp. "She's scheduled for a hysterectomy in the morning. Ma, can you come home?"

"I can't come home now. You know I work, and besides that, I hate to fly."

I waited for her to say something that would improve the situation—something hopeful, something that would untie the knot in my stomach.

"Call me when the surgery is over. Danielle, she's going to be okay. Your sister is a strong girl."

I felt relieved when I hung up, but I would have felt better knowing that my mother was coming to Karole's bedside.

Phil and I sat in the hospital's waiting room, each minute exaggerated by the clock ticking on the wall. When it seemed like an eternity had passed, I glanced at the clock again to discover that only a few minutes had passed.

I thought of Gilda Radner, the comedian Karole and I adored. She died recently from ovarian cancer. Karole and I talked about her after she passed, and I could still recall our conversation. We couldn't believe Gilda had died at only forty-two years old. I sarcastically laughed to myself. Gilda was right about one thing… "It's always something."

Karole is only thirty-two. I stayed calm and did not let Phil know the turmoil that was screaming in my head. *She might die.* I wished I had a paper bag to breathe into.

The doors swung open several hours later, and Karole's surgeon walked in. He spotted Phil and then walked toward us. He was an older man, the fatherly type. His surgical mask hung below his chin, and he wore a serious expression. Phil and I jumped to our feet.

"The surgery went well. The pathology confirmed our suspicions… Karole has ovarian cancer."

"You mean she *had* ovarian cancer," I corrected him. "You got it all, right?"

"There's no way to know if the cancer has spread," he said kindly. "Her uterus seemed to be free of cancer, and I didn't see any metastasis in her nearby organs."

"What does that mean?" Phil asked.

"It means that I did not see that the cancer had spread. I sent lymph nodes to pathology to be tested, and we'll know more when those results come back."

"So, what happens now?" I asked. Medical terminology might as well have been a foreign language. I held a notebook and wrote down anything I didn't understand.

"Karole will have to see an oncologist, of course, but I think we caught it early."

I hugged the doctor's neck and thanked him for doing the surgery, and Phil vigorously shook his hand.

An hour later, a nurse entered the waiting room. Karole was awake and ready to see visitors.

"The nurse just gave me a pain shot," Karole said as we entered her room. "I just want to sleep."

"Go to sleep, sweetheart," Phil said as he pushed her hair from her face.

Her lips began to quiver, and in a rare moment, her eyes filled with tears. "Phil," she said in a crackling voice, "I can't have babies."

Phil wiped her eyes with a tissue. "We don't need babies, silly girl. We've got each other," he said kindly.

I thanked God for Phil. After the horrors of our childhood, Phil had been Karole's savior. I wondered if I would ever meet someone so kind and caring. But at that moment, all that mattered to me was that Karole had found a good man who loved her with all his heart.

I pulled a chair to her bedside and took her hand.

"Karole… Are you feeling any pain?"

"No. I feel wonderful after the pain shot."

"Go to sleep, sister. I will pray for you."

"Bible thumper," she whispered with a husky laugh; it was one of her favorite nicknames for me. Throughout the years, I encouraged her to read the Bible. I could never discern if she had faith in God, and whenever I mentioned a higher power, she appeared uneasy and shifted the conversation.

THIRTY-ONE

Looking Back

I WAS NOT equipped to deal with what happened to me. I didn't understand the magnitude or gravity of what my father did to me. He used emotional leverage and extortion to get what he wanted. He manipulated me like a puppet and held me captive.

The day I entered the woods with my father, my life was already in disarray. If he had not abused me that day, I strongly suspect I would have suffered emotional wounds; I was uneducated and had been kept hidden from the world. Even without the introduction of sexual abuse in my life, how would I have grown to be a productive member of society?

If nothing more had changed that day and the status quo remained, I would have had difficulty making a life for myself as an adult. But the status quo did change that day, forcing me into an even darker world. I emerged from the woods in Goodlettsville, Tennessee, a different version of the girl who had entered.

My father loved Karole above everyone else except himself, and it took most of my life to understand why. It had nothing to do with Karole being unique; it had everything to do with Karole being available.

I wasn't stupid, lazy, or useless. The sexual abuse started at age fifteen, but before that, I was mentally abused as he prepared me for a future of sexual abuse. He realized that Karole would someday be gone, and I would take her place.

If the universe operates in a way that will someday allow me to communicate with my father, I have a list of questions prepared for him... Why were you so angry, and did you feel better about yourself by making others suffer? When you closed your eyes to sleep, did you think about what you did to your daughters? Did you genuinely believe you were teaching us something or that we deserved the abuse? Were you aware that we had feelings? Did you know you were ruining our lives? Did you care? Were you sorry for what you did when you were on your deathbed?

If my mother knew what he was doing to us, why didn't she stop him? Why didn't she take her two young daughters and return to her siblings in Hornepayne? Someone would have made room for us, and knowing what I have recently learned, they would have welcomed us back with open arms. She had many opportunities to escape when he left us on one of his extended business trips.

When my father "punished" me for sucking my fingers when I was a toddler, my mother nearly gave me up for adoption. Why didn't she take my sister and me and leave then? I never learned what he did to me, but I suspect she saw that he was a sexual deviant and forgave him after he promised to change.

Did she think what he did was a one-time thing? Or did she turn a blind eye and sacrifice her daughters to save her marriage? Was my mother the perfect angel I always thought her to be? Or was she a flawed human being?

What was so special about my father that made my mother willing to cross Canada and the United States countless times? How did he explain the necessity of changing their surname in every town and keeping their daughters hidden and uneducated?

After my father died, I thought my mother would explain why our family was always on the run. She seemed to know more than she let on, and I felt I deserved to know the truth. I refrained from pressing her for answers and hoped she would explain everything when she felt ready, but she never did.

I also have a list of questions for my mother... At what point did you become aware of your husband's sordid past? Did your religious beliefs prevent you from defying him? Were you afraid to leave him? Did he threaten you? Or were you so in love with him that you stayed in the relationship... despite everything? Were you ever aware that he was sexually abusing Karole and me? Did you seriously intend to give me up for adoption to save your marriage?

I want to believe that my father told my mother on their wedding night, "Theresa, I had a wife and two daughters in my past, and I was afraid you wouldn't marry me if I told you." I want to think she loved him so much that she forgave him. I want to believe he never told my mother he raped his daughter and beat his former brother-in-law until he thought he had killed him.

Statistically, the chances of Karole surviving beyond five years after the diagnosis of ovarian cancer were slim in the 1980s. After her hysterectomy, Karole and Phil talked about the idea of adopting a child, and I even offered to carry a baby for her. However, Karole was worried that she wouldn't be a good parent, and the fear of her cancer returning always lingered in her mind. As a result, they remained childless.

After two decades of marriage, Karole revealed the secrets of our childhood to Phil. He felt deeply saddened for her and wished she had confided in him earlier. In some ways, her confession explained a lot. She had spent a lifetime in and out of depression, and he now understood the reason. Phil had spent a significant amount of time with our father before his death and looked back with regret. Had he known, he would have treated my father very differently.

Karole fought a lifelong battle with an eating disorder. She worked as an optician's assistant until she became disabled in her late fifties. When the time came to apply for disability compensation, Karole had to search for her birth certificate. After over a year of searching, she found it located in Quebec.

Karole was born "Baby Deslinières" on September 25, 1957, and I was born "Danielle King" fourteen months later. Neither one of us was given our father's valid surname, Parise. My parents were married with the surname of Bouchard... They had been concealing their identities since the beginning of their marriage.

Complications from the eating disorder were what ultimately took Karole's life at age sixty-five. Phil was by her side until the end.

My sister and I remained close throughout our adult lives. I lived across the country, but we talked as often as possible. Many years had passed since the abuse, but once in a while, we'd discuss it until we could speak no more. Without my sister to support me, I don't know how I would have survived. And without me to support Karole, I believe she would have died years earlier.

I see two paths to choose from after growing up in an abusive family: You can either perpetuate the cycle of abuse (directed toward yourself, others, or both), or you can use the experience to learn and strive to make things better.

I looked back on the struggles of my early life with a singular aim: to find others experiencing similar challenges. Someone sharing this message with me or circumventing my father could have led my life down a different path. Children facing chronic abuse often feel trapped, unaware that they have alternatives; they lack a reference point to understand that their experiences are not typical.

A family that doesn't blend into the neighborhood and whose children walk with their heads down is not normal, and children who stay inside their homes are not typical. Some people looked upon my sister and me sorrowfully but didn't take it further. They didn't want to become involved. It isn't easy to intervene in these situations.

Occasionally, neighbors inquired but backed off once my father's anger confronted them. I wish those neighbors had taken their curiosity further and notified the authorities. I don't harbor ill feelings toward those who didn't help us; how could they have known what was happening? And mistakenly accusing someone of sexual abuse is a slippery slope. It could ruin a life.

It would have helped if my mother's or father's extended family had stepped in. However, they had no way of locating us. Karole and I were tossed into a sea of abuse, and it was sink or swim. There were no life preservers in sight.

So much can be said in hindsight… "They were the quiet family," "I saw bruises on the children," "They didn't mingle with anyone." "Their shades were always drawn…" Hindsight is always 20/20.

Sexual abuse from a family member happens too often, but sexual abuse from one's biological father is rare. I thought I was alone in my struggles. I was kept mentally beaten down, and anytime I gained a sense of pride or accomplishment, my father put me back in my place.

My father uprooted us at the drop of a hat, so maybe our family was beyond help. Even if the proper authorities had been notified, we'd have been gone when they arrived. We would have left everything behind—and not given anyone a clue about where we were heading.

I had been groomed all my life to be submissive, so when the time was right, it was easy to take advantage of me. My childhood lifestyle set me up for an unusual life.

When I finally left home at twenty-three, I possessed the maturity of a teenager. I was prepared to fight to be the best at anything I did. I was wound tightly and convinced that being competitive—a force to be reckoned with—was the only way to survive.

I've been told I am too soft-hearted for most of my adult life, but I wasn't always soft-hearted. In my twenties and thirties, I was overly competitive and did whatever it took to reach my goals. It didn't bother me to lie to get the promotion or turn my back on a coworker who also wanted the job. Life was a competition, and I believed that if I worked at top speed, I would become successful. I learned from my father... success at any cost. Think only of yourself. Nobody else matters.

My mother had planted seeds of spirituality in me at an early age, and when I reached my mid-thirties, those seeds started to grow. I wasn't happy with the way I had been living. Success at any cost was not who I was. I was no longer sexually abused, but the remnants of the abuse still ruled my life.

At age thirty-three, I married for a second time. My second husband, Lee, was the Pro Shop manager at the bowling alley where I worked—the same man who constantly complained to me about his wife. He had a young son but had no contact with him.

When we got married, Lee appeared ambitious, but over time, I realized he favored a more relaxed approach to life. I started to question whether my strong work ethic was a disadvantage; the men in my life could unwind while I cared for everything myself. I juggled a job and managed the household independently, without assistance from anyone.

For years, he drank every evening to the point of drunkenness, and his drug addiction was impossible to ignore. He was perpetually angry at the world and took it out on me. He'd scream at the top of his lungs, just inches from my face, for all the neighbors to hear.

Lee and I repeated the same scenario many times... Fed up with his drug use and laziness, I would leave him. He then threatened or feebly attempted suicide, and I would return to him out of guilt. It hurt my heart to see the pitiful look on his face. How could I leave a man who needed my help? What would people think of a woman who didn't return to a man who needed her?

Over the years, I have had many jobs. I trained and groomed dogs, was a nursing assistant, wrote service manuals for an auto repair business, and sold cars. I was a cook and a restaurant manager. I did housekeeping. I worked in high school cafeterias. I picked strawberries and onions. I took any job to pay the bills.

In the late 90s, Lee and I managed a storage rental facility. I took all the bookings, collected the monthly rental checks, cleaned out the units when customers failed to pay, and took care of the grounds... while Lee golfed, fished, and hung out with his friends.

Finding myself pregnant at thirty-nine terrified me. I cried for days. I didn't have a maternal bone in my body. What kind of parent would I be? Did my upbringing ruin my chances of being a good mother? What kind of father would Lee be?

I argued with my husband for weeks to make him understand that he needed to get his drug and alcohol use under control. He was going to be a father again. He had an estranged son from his first marriage; this was an opportunity for him to be a better father. He finally agreed.

I lacked experience with babies and didn't know how to care for one. Fortunately, my recent job as a

CNA at a nursing home equipped me with essential skills. I learned to change diapers and ensure the patients were fed and clean. The training proved invaluable.

As my stomach swelled, I put my hand on it, trying to elicit love, care, or concern—something motherly. But I felt nothing. It was only a lump that made me nauseous every morning.

After twenty hours of labor, my son Dustin was born. I looked at his little face when the nurse handed him to me. He was helpless. I brought him into the world, and it suddenly became clear that I would need to protect him. He became the center of my world. He was the first thing I thought of every morning, and everything I did was for him.

I oversaw Dustin's education and tried to shield him from the trouble between me and his father. I taught him from an early age what inappropriate touching was and told him that if it ever happened to him, he was to run screaming for help in the opposite direction. Once I became a mother, I knew that if anyone brought harm to my child, they would have me to contend with, and they might want to run for their life.

My life with Lee was difficult as, once again, I married a man who depended on my salary to survive and had little interest in gainful employment.

For several years in Albuquerque, Lee's drug use was managed. We purchased a dilapidated house, transformed our garage into a wood shop, and took up the hobby of building and refinishing furniture. Dustin was a teenager who did well in school and had many friends. I found fulfillment in raising Dustin and pursuing my woodworking hobby, and I convinced myself that it was enough to sustain a happy life.

I hadn't looked at my father's articles since I received them from my cousin Dottie twenty years earlier. Dustin, now a teenager, never had a relationship with a grandparent; he had met my mother only a handful of times.

I bought a scrapbook and inserted the articles, creating a memory book for my son of the grandfather, whom he never knew.

Dustin took an interest in reading the articles his grandfather had written about his adventures in the war. I spoke to my son about my father in a positive manner. What could it hurt? His grandfather had served in the war and was wounded, and he deserved credit for that. I focused on what he had done for his country—for my son's sake.

In 2013, a man who was fleeing the police at 100 miles per hour ran a red light and T-boned our car on the driver's side. Lee was driving, and I was the passenger.

I remember crunching sounds and glass falling around me. I lost all sense of gravity as the car tumbled. Then, dead silence. The next thing I remember is being transported to the hospital in an ambulance. Lee was on a cot beside me, and there was a lot of blood. A paramedic was leaning over him. I screamed my husband's name, but there was no response. I felt excruciating pain in every cell of my body before falling back into unconsciousness.

The next thing I remember is waking up after surgery. I asked the nurse about my husband.

"Your husband is still in surgery," she said sympathetically.

"Why does everything hurt?" I asked the nurse.

"You just had surgery for a ruptured bladder, and your pelvis is broken. You also have a subdural hematoma."

"What does that mean?" I asked.

"You have bleeding in your brain from the impact."

The following morning, I got news of Lee. He was out of surgery. All of his ribs on the left were broken, and he had lost his left lung. He also had a broken pelvis and a subdural hematoma, and he was in a coma.

I was discharged from the hospital ten days later and then spent several days in rehab. Lee slowly regained consciousness.

His injuries were severe, and the nurses were never able to get his pain under control. I asked his nurse if his history of drug abuse made the pain medications he received useless. She thanked me for my honesty and said she'd ask the doctor if they could increase his dosages.

Before the accident, Lee craved drugs and alcohol, but afterward, his focus turned to chasing an even greater high. Lee told me that the entire time he was in a coma, the devil was sitting at his bedside.

Lee filed a lawsuit against the police department for pursuing a perpetrator through a densely populated area.

We were called to court to testify. On the witness stand, the defense lawyer asked me if Lee was addicted to drugs, to which I answered, "Yes." He then asked me if Lee was under the influence of drugs or alcohol the day of the accident…

"I don't believe he took drugs or drank when he drove." I wanted to believe my words, but in truth, I had no way of knowing.

Lee chased the lawsuit for years; I couldn't take the stress anymore and begged him to drop it. It was a dead end. He lived and breathed in a state of anger and revenge. Our lawyer could find no evidence to prove the perpetrator ran a red light. It was the city versus us, and Lee's reputation for drug use was all the defense needed to laugh us out of court.

During one of the court proceedings, the man who hit us was in the courtroom. He had served only months in prison for his crimes. I watched him out of the corner of my eye. I couldn't look away—this man had changed our lives forever. When the proceedings ended, I approached him.

"I am the woman who was in the car you crashed into," I stated clearly. "I want you to know my husband and I will never be the same… You could have killed us. You got $200 from the home you robbed… Was it worth it?" I looked for sympathy in his eyes but saw only a blank stare. I went on. "You changed our lives forever."

He walked away. I wanted to touch his heart in some way, but years later learned he was involved in another home invasion.

After my mother left for Canada in 1989, she returned to visit Karole and me a handful of times. As she aged, I begged her to live with me and let me care for her, but her answer was a firm, "No."

Over time, my mother distanced herself from my sister and me, leaving our relationship almost nonexistent. Ultimately, she preferred to be with her siblings.

In 2015, she was diagnosed with bone cancer and was given months to live. Again, I pleaded with her to allow me to care for her in her final days, but she declined my offer. I'm unsure what she communicated to her siblings, but they requested that Karole and I keep our distance during her final days.

I never held any resentment toward my aunts and uncles for keeping Karole and me at arm's length during my mother's illness; they were only honoring my mother's wishes. After my father died, my mother chose to distance herself from us. It broke my heart to adapt to life without her, yet I had no choice but to move forward.

Karole and I were notified by Aunt Ann when our mother passed away, but not one of her siblings reached out to comfort us. We weren't invited to her funeral, our names were absent from her will, and we were not acknowledged as her children.

Soon after my mother's passing, Karole and I were contacted by our cousins Terri and Michelle (the cousins who had lost their mother and brother in a car crash in 1971). We hadn't seen them since we were children. We had a long conversation about my mother's final days. They felt it was wrong for the elders in our family not to include us in the funeral arrangements. Shortly after, they came to Albuquerque to visit my sister and me. My sister and I shared stories of our confusing childhood, missing years, and why we had disappeared from their lives.

In his late twenties, Dustin fell in love with Cassandra, a charming young woman, and they married. They relocated to Wisconsin to be near her family. A year later, Lee and I sold our home in Albuquerque and relocated to Wisconsin to be nearer to our son and his wife.

Lee's demons continued to grow. He wanted "everyone to suffer," which included me and our son. He grabbed a shotgun from a closet, racked it, and said, "I'm going to shoot up the neighborhood and blow the walls out of this apartment!" Then added… "You would be fun to kill, Danielle!"

I ran from the house with my cell phone and called the police. A SWAT team arrived shortly, cuffed him, and took him away. Two weeks later, he was released from a mental health facility. The doctor said they had cured him. I didn't want him back, but he was a sickly man, and soft-hearted me began to feel the all-too-familiar guilt. I called my son and asked him to get the gun out of the house… His father was coming home.

The doctors couldn't have been more wrong. Lee was far from cured and even more hostile when he returned home. Shortly after, I discovered a hunting knife in the drawer of his bedside table—it had never been there before. Fearing he planned to kill me in my sleep, I ran out of the house with only my car keys (he hid my phone) and returned several hours later with a police officer at my side to collect my belongings and my dog. I could never go back. I moved in with my son and his wife.

THIRTY-TWO

Full Circle

AFTER LEAVING LEE, my life was quieter than it had been for thirty-seven years. I had time to read the Bible, pray for the future, and reflect upon my past.

My life has been anything but typical. Growing up with an abusive father influenced my choice of partners. My first husband, Jess, was much older than me, which felt normal at the time since my mother had also married an older man. However, in hindsight, I realize Jess and I might have been better off as friends. While we had many joyful moments together, I often questioned if my feelings for him were rooted in love or if I viewed him as a father figure.

After marrying Lee, I faced all the challenges he brought into my life. Living with him felt like riding a turbulent roller coaster—far from enjoyable. I constantly dealt with his temper and his addictions. I might have left if he had ever harmed me physically, but he didn't. He often confronted me aggressively and belittled me, making sure I understood who was in charge, and he reacted negatively if I dared to question him. Being "seen but not heard" was nothing new, and I could manage it. I had grown used to a life filled with ups and downs. While others might have fled from a relationship like ours, I accepted this lifestyle gracefully and humbly.

Life is never perfect, and I would never strive for perfection. But looking back, I began to see a pattern. I was raised in an atmosphere of abuse; I had nothing to compare my life to. I was expected to work my fingers to the bone, and I did.

I cherished Jess during our marriage, and my heart shattered when he revealed his affair. I initially loved Lee, but that affection dwindled rapidly, leading me to remain with him simply out of habit.

Even though I was able to escape from the abuse of my father, I never freed myself. I persisted in my life, repeating the same destructive patterns but involving different people and forms of abuse. My past still imprisoned me, and it was time to liberate myself.

One of my favorite Bible quotes is, "I can do all things through Him who strengthens me." God occasionally whispers to me, but at other times, He has to raise His voice when I believe my actions are paramount.

Sometimes, a gift is as simple as the person standing next to me in the grocery checkout line who says something profound that resonates for the rest of the day. A gift can be a text message from a friend that touches my heart or my dog as she cuddles on my lap. Maybe someone from my past calls out of the blue, or I feel the sun's warmth shining on my face. The gifts given to me come in different packages; the difference now is that I recognize them.

We can choose between good and evil, be active or passive, decide or hesitate. We can aid others or focus solely on ourselves. We can opt to enhance our lives or remain stagnant, neglecting the gifts we've received. Numerous kind individuals have supported me throughout my healing journey, and all I had to do was ask God for them to enter my life.

My son and his wife have been my biggest supporters during my difficulties with my husband, and I will be forever grateful. Guided by their love, I envision a future in which abuse and control hold no more power over me.

People have always told me to "write a book," but I didn't want to rehash the painful memories. How would I ever sort through the confusion? But didn't I owe it to myself to move forward and live the way God intended for me?

I kept in touch with my cousins Terri and Michelle after they visited Karole and me in Albuquerque. We kept each other informed of weddings and funerals and sent Christmas cards, but I couldn't help but wonder if they held a key to help me find some answers.

I called Terri and Michelle and explained that I was thinking a lot about my childhood and was going through a difficult time in my marriage. I had many decisions ahead of me.

Several days later, I received a text message from Michelle...

"Hi, Danielle! Terri and I want to offer you a chance to get away. We would love for you to come and stay with us for a visit for as long as you want. We could arrange a get-together with the family. I know they would be thrilled to see you! Sometimes, spending time away with people who love you can do wonders for the soul. You have spent your whole life caring for

others; now is the perfect time to be on the receiving end!"

My cousins were excitedly planning our activities for my visit. Upon my arrival, we would celebrate Uncle Camille's birthday with a surprise party, spend a weekend at a cottage in Lac Simon, Chénéville, Quebec, enjoy time at a beauty salon, and visit other relatives. Their enthusiasm was contagious, and I eagerly anticipated the trip.

Terri and Michelle greeted me with warm hugs as I exited the plane.

"Oh my goodness,… Has anyone ever told you that you look almost exactly like my Grandmother Laura? I'm sorry, I mean *our* Grandmother Laura? The resemblance is striking! I didn't notice it when I last saw you ten years ago."

"Well, my hair has turned gray, so that might have something to do with it." I laughed. "My mother may have mentioned the resemblance to me when I was a little girl, but I only met our grandmother a few times."

We talked continuously throughout the hour-long ride. They shared insights about their lives while I discussed the brighter moments from mine. They highlighted how our family had plans to keep me occupied during my two-week visit. I felt like I was home.

The first few days were spent visiting my cousins and their spouses. Everyone commented on my resemblance to our grandmother, and they had to stop and study my face for a moment before looking at one another in astonishment.

I watched as Uncle Camille got out of the car. He looked like the man I remembered from childhood, except sixty years older. No one had told him I was coming; I was part of the surprise.

About thirty family members approached him and cheered, "Surprise!" Then, someone placed a "Happy 90th Birthday" hat on his head. His face lit up as he walked toward the picnic table, which was decorated for his birthday, and held dish after dish of delicious food. The group burst into the "Happy Birthday" song.

"Uncle Camille," one of my cousins said, "we have another surprise for you!" He looked momentarily stunned, unable to imagine what more his family had in store. The group around him stepped to the side to reveal me. His jaw dropped. His mouth moved, but no words came out.

"Uncle Camille, this is Danielle,... your sister Theresa's daughter," someone explained. "She flew in from Wisconsin to help celebrate your birthday!"

"Hello, Uncle Camille!" I approached him slowly. He opened his arms and embraced me.

"Danielle," he said, his voice cracking as he hugged me, smiling as if he had been saving that smile all his life for when we would meet again.

"Danielle, you're here! This is amazing!" he exclaimed as he studied my face.

"Let's sit down. I'm an old man now!" He spoke in a beautiful French Canadian accent—my mother's accent—with the same cheerful lilt I remembered from childhood.

The large group gathered around the picnic table, filled their plates, and reminisced about Uncle Camille's life. My cheeks began to ache from smiling and laughing.

I can count on one hand how many times I've met my mother's family. I never had the chance to form the connections they enjoyed. These individuals had spent their lives together, celebrating birthdays, holidays, and hockey games—experiences I completely missed. Yet, they embraced me back into the family, filling my heart with love. They took special care to ensure I felt comfortable and accepted. These beautiful, loving people had always been waiting for me.

After everyone had their fill of cake, they moved on to other activities, leaving Uncle Camille and me alone at the table.

"Has anyone ever told you that you are a clone of my mother? Your grandmother? I was astonished when I first saw you."

"Yes, that's been mentioned a few times since I arrived."

I was proud to resemble my grandmother. Somehow, it made me feel that I was one of them and had the right to be there with my mother's family... with my family.

"How are you?" he asked sincerely, his eyes piercing mine. Someone had made him aware of my past.

"I'm doing okay," I answered with a forced cheer and a nod.

"I'm glad to hear that. I understand you had a terrible childhood, and that breaks my heart. I have thought of you a million times over the years. I've always wondered where you were."

"We were everywhere," I answered with a nervous laugh. "My childhood was a confusing time."

"Well, you're with us now, and we won't lose you again!" He put his arm around me and hugged me, then went on…

"Danielle, I tried to tell your mother not to marry your father, but she wouldn't listen. Jack and I attended catechism lessons together. I was there for confirmation, and he was there to convert to Catholicism. I saw something in him that wasn't right. I sensed that he was mechanically going through the lessons, but his heart wasn't in it. The fact that he was so much older than your mother greatly concerned me. I asked him about his past, but he was vague with his answers. I pushed to learn more about him, but curiosity only irritated him. I caught him in several lies, too."

"Well, Uncle Camille, you were right. He *was* hiding something."

"We found your family on Christmas Day in 1967 and surprised you all. Do you remember that day, Danielle?"

"Yes, that was one of the best days of my life!"

"A few weeks later, a cop showed up at my door and asked questions about your father. I got scared and denied knowing his whereabouts. I called your father immediately and warned him that the police were looking for him. Danielle, I should have told that cop where your father was. I have regretted that decision every day since. Right after that, your family vanished off the face of the earth. And now I understand that you and your sister had a terrible childhood… and it's my fault." His voice cracked, and his eyes filled with tears. At that moment, I knew my Uncle Camille was another casualty of my father's actions.

"No! It's not your fault, Uncle Camille!" I reached out and took his hand. "It wasn't all bad. Once, we lived on a ranch in Athabaska with twenty horses, and Karole and I were wranglers! We even lived on Vancouver Island near the beach!"

"But, Danielle, you never went to school," he said sadly.

"I went to first and second grade. I read hundreds of books growing up, probably more than other kids my age. And I taught myself everything I needed to know," I reassured him.

He stared off into the distance as he recalled a memory... "Your grandmother sat by a window every evening and prayed for your mother and you two girls. She prayed for over thirty years and finally stopped when your mother returned to her after your father passed away."

During childhood, I often felt isolated. If I had known my grandmother was praying for me, it would have meant everything.

On my final day in Canada, my cousin Tania and her husband invited me to dinner at their home. To my surprise, they gave me three sweatshirts embroidered with "Oh, Canada"—one for me, one for my son, and one for my daughter-in-law.

While spending time with my cousins, they welcomed me with open arms and shared their best guidance. They emphasized the importance of self-respect and self-love. They reassured me that my happiness was solely my responsibility and that no one else could fulfill it. They urged me to commit to counseling. They reminded me that our mothers were watching over us from Heaven, providing me with the strength to overcome the abuse I had suffered. They, along with God, would help me find a resolution that was in my best interest.

They urged me to remain steadfast with my husband and voiced worries about my safety. They empowered me to recognize my strength and reminded me that I deserved happiness. They praised my resilience and assured me of their love, stating that their doors would always be open to me.

During my visit, one of my cousins asked me, "When was the last time Lee made you happy?" I was stunned by the question and had to think about it for days. I was never able to answer her question.

In addition to their kind words, something else became apparent... All my cousins were married to men who treated them with respect. Each husband spoke to his wife with kindness. I saw couples looking at one another with affectionate gazes, and it moved me to see men express such emotions. It was both beautiful and overwhelming, leaving me struggling to understand.

I doubt my Canadian family will ever realize the depth of love I experienced while with them. Despite the years I was away, they somehow made me feel like I never left.

THIRTY-THREE

Looking Forward

IN MY MID-FORTIES, one of my three jobs involved cleaning houses. I brought a radio to enjoy my favorite Christian station while I passed the time. I had a goal—to deepen my faith, even joining Calvary Church in Albuquerque, hoping that would be a good start. I had been praying throughout my life but felt spiritually unfulfilled and needed help to progress.

That day, I put all my energy into scrubbing the floor. I wanted my clients to be satisfied with my services. My reputation for being a hard worker and a good employee preceded me, and I took pride in my work.

As I listened to Christian music, I spoke with Jesus. I asked for His help to forget my past and wipe away my memories. I wanted to start a new chapter of my life, and I wanted a clean slate! My marriage was challenging, but I felt equipped to handle that. The memories of the abuse tormented me and were much more complicated. I longed for them to vanish, no longer hitting me with the dawn of each new day.

Being a mother brought me the greatest joy of my life. I had learned how to keep Lee's problems from our son, and as far as I could tell, Dustin was a happy, well-adjusted six-year-old boy who loved trucks, bugs, and first grade. It wasn't hard to put Dustin's needs before my own. I knew I would give my life without hesitation to save him.

My mother was not affectionate toward me and my sister when we were children unless my father was away on a business trip. That always puzzled me, but I finally realized she was aloof toward us because my father would become jealous; her affection was reserved only for him.

Hugging Dustin when he came home from school didn't come naturally to me, and I had to remind myself to do it. I wasn't the mother who fawned over her child; I may have treated him more like an adult than a little boy. As Dustin grew, Lee became the strict disciplinarian, and I was the softie ready to step in and shield Dustin from Lee's temper.

Why, with the joy of raising my son, was I still suffering? Why couldn't I stop picturing the abuse in my mind? As the years passed, my memories became more intense instead of fading like I had expected.

The Christian rock music kept my hands moving. The singers praised God for His glory; sometimes, I sang along. I wanted to be moved by the music but wasn't feeling it. Was that part of me broken as well?

I threw my sponge into the bucket. Frustrated, I wondered where was the redemption the songs promised? I had been attending church every Sunday and listening to the Christian radio station ad nauseam, but I felt nothing; I was going through the motions.

I looked up toward the ceiling.

"God, I'm grateful for all the blessings you've given me. But I can't get the memories out of my head, and I can't get the hatred out of my heart!" I choked up as I spoke into the empty room. "Are you even listening to me? Are you even there?!"

I scrubbed harder as the singers praised the Lord. But instead of feeling moved, I was irritated. Where was the relief the music should bring? Where were the answers I needed? Where was the happiness that everyone else seemed to be enjoying?

"God, why is my life so hard!" I yelled into the room.

I felt momentarily ashamed. Did God hear me? Is He angry at me for my harsh words?

I took my bucket to the backyard to dump the dirty water. A flock of red-winged blackbirds sang in the distance—a sure sign of spring. I stood straight, filled my lungs with fresh air, then looked at the sky and whispered.

"I'm sorry. You have a plan for me, but I wish I knew it." I returned to the house and refilled my bucket at the kitchen sink.

I put the radio on the bathroom counter. As I started to scrub again, a preacher began talking about forgiveness. I considered switching to a rock station, but my hands were wet. I continued working to get the job done and listened half-heartedly.

"What if the person who hurt you has never asked to be forgiven? You're ridiculous!" I said sarcastically to the radio as I scrubbed furiously.

"Forgive others," the preacher said, "not because they deserve forgiveness, but because you deserve peace." I stopped scrubbing and sat with my back against the tub. *What did he say?*

"Forgiveness is about empowering yourself rather than letting your past empower you. Without forgiveness, your life will be governed by an endless cycle of resentment and retaliation. Blame keeps wounds open. Forgiveness allows wounds to heal. **Never is the human soul so strong as when it relinquishes revenge and dares to forgive an injustice!**"

I sat perfectly still; I did not want to miss the preacher's words.

"Pope John Paul the Second has said, **'Forgiveness is, above all, a personal choice, a decision of the heart to go against the natural instinct to pay back evil with evil!'**"

Will I be free if I forgive my father? Will I be happy? Is it as simple as that?

Maybe *I* needed forgiveness... I chose not to tell my mother or inform the authorities. Was that a sin? I stopped fighting him, and I accepted the abuse as my way of life. Was that a sin? I carried hatred in my heart for my father since that fateful day in the woods when it all began, and I have wished him dead every day since. Was that a sin? Who did I need to apologize to? And who would forgive me?!

The preacher continued...

"Forgiveness is the powerful expression of the love within your soul. To forgive is not a feeling. It's a commitment you make every day. It's your choice to show mercy and not hold the offense against the offender. Forgiveness is the ultimate expression of love within our souls. **If you want to know love, you must forgive.**"

Forgiving my father had never entered my mind. Revenge, yes. Forgiveness, no. How do you forgive someone who has never apologized? I never saw a moment of sorrow in his eyes. And not for a moment did I see a modicum of remorse.

With my father's death, I thought there would be peace. All my life, I believed that the instant he died, I would be dancing on clouds, deliriously happy. But that feeling never came. When he took his last breath, he closed his eyes, and nothing else changed.

"Forgive," I whispered to hear the sound of the word. The word was foreign to my ears as if it were the first time I had heard it.

"Jesus," my words echoed in the empty room. "You died to take away the sin of the world… Did you forgive my father? Is he in Heaven with you?" my voice cracked.

I felt a warmth as if someone had wrapped loving arms around me. The frustration I had felt earlier had eased.

"He had a hole in his soul," I stated, not knowing where the words originated.

I buried my face in my hands. Never before had I considered forgiveness. I will never forget what my father did, but I felt a new world opening for me as I relinquished my anger.

"I forgive you, Daddy… I forgive you…" I cried into the empty room.

The preacher on the radio was correct: forgiveness isn't a one-time thing—it's a commitment, a way of life. From that day on the bathroom floor, I have made the conscious decision to live in a state of forgiveness. I was wounded, but the wound has healed, and I bear a scar.

I didn't forgive my father for each time he hurt me; I forgave every trespass against me at once. He committed a series of sins. He was flawed; he lived his life thinking only of himself and his needs. I forgave him for being who he was.

Forgiving him did not make what he did to me right. It did not cause me to see him in a different light, nor did I wear rose-tinted glasses and pretend everything that happened was okay. Forgiving freed me from the anger in my heart and allowed me to move forward without the burden of hate. Forgiving softened me, awakened me to the gifts I have been given, and let me find my voice, believe in myself, and recognize my free will.

I had always thought I was abnormal, but by living in a state of forgiveness, I now understand that *what happened* to me was abnormal. I was put in an impossible situation. I was dealt a losing hand... I played a game of solitaire with no moves or choices. Nobody said, "Go this way" or "Try this instead." I was perpetually facing a brick wall I could not climb over or go around.

Abusers use their free will to harm others, and we may never understand why. But they cannot be allowed to ruin our lives—we can't give our abuser that power over us.

People often ask me how I still love my father, a man who gave me little reason to love him. My answer is: If Jesus can forgive the world, I can forgive one man. I cannot love others if I carry the burden of hate in my heart, and I want to feel love! That's all I've ever wanted.

My father is in a different place now, and it is not up to me to judge him any longer. I pray he begged for forgiveness and was granted it, but his fate is in the hands of a much greater power, and it's not mine to question.

Witnessing my son become a responsible young man and a caring husband has been the joy of my life. When I became pregnant, my marriage was struggling, and I didn't feel prepared for motherhood. Lacking the skills to be a nurturing parent, I learned as I went along, with Dustin as my guide.

I've learned that people don't necessarily need to be blood-related to become family. I've chosen my heart's sisters and brothers; I know they'll be with me until the end. They check on me often and tell me I'm in their prayers.

Then there's little Katie, my long-haired dachshund. I'm convinced Katie is an earth angel here to ensure I feel loved every minute of the day. She watches me with soulful eyes, and when the day is done, she climbs up on my lap and gently pushes my book down with her paw if I'm not giving her enough attention. Her happiness depends on knowing she's made me laugh (and an occasional treat). She's not an ordinary dog, and it's no coincidence that D-O-G is G-O-D spelled backward.

My extended family accepted me back into their lives with open arms. My Canadian relatives' texts and phone calls are now a typical part of my life. They know many details of my past and love me all the more for it. Their continued support amazes me more with each passing day.

Leaving Lee was inevitable. As I grew, I saw him as an extension of the person I was, but I am no longer. We no longer fit together. I've learned to surround myself with people who love me, not those who use me.

I reflected on the pain of my past for a purpose: to inspire hope! If sharing my journey enables even one person to rise above the traumas of abuse, then it will have been worthwhile. It took me years to stop justifying my father's actions. Finally, the day arrived when I needed to proclaim my message from the rooftops.

I still smile at the memory of my sister calling me a "Bible thumper." I wanted Karole to see my path, believing it would aid our souls in healing. Though I think she grasped my intentions, her stoic nature prevented her from acknowledging it.

Karole and I came from the same family, but our journeys were uniquely our own. I feel peace in the knowledge that she is in a better place, released from the torment she lived with every moment of every day. She now knows the answers that I have yet to learn.

I'm not rushing to join her; I've received countless blessings I wish to savor. Still, I hope Karole will be there to greet me, wrapping her protective arm around me as she explains everything. Perhaps my parents will be present, too, sharing the reasons behind everything, finally making it all clear. Maybe there's no room for resentment in Heaven—only love remains.

"Danielle"

Please return to Amazon, and
Write a Review!

Help spread the word…

**AFTER ABUSE,
THERE IS HOPE, LIFE, AND LOVE!**

Thank you,

K. D. Kinz

GOOD MORNING, DEAR GOD

What awaits me this day?
Please, show me exquisite joy,
so my heart leaps
Let me feel empathy,
so my heart cries
Let those around me feel love
Amid the commotion of the day,
I appreciate the song of the birds,
a smile from a stranger,
the warmth of the sun,
the music that surrounds me
Thank You for the food I will eat,
the water I will drink
Remind me to care for the Earth,
to care for myself,
to move and to sweat
I am here to learn,
though some lessons are difficult
You are in me; we are One
Through my eyes, my voice, my actions, You witness my life
You are not only with me
when I cry for You
I can never send You away
You are the blood flowing through my veins
In the noise of the day,
let me hear Your voice
Speak loudly, as I can be selfish and distracted
I want to go through every room in my home,
every room in my heart,
sweep out what is unnecessary,
then fill the void
with the light of You

Help me realize everyone I love will slip through my fingers
and return to You,
By returning to You,
they return to me
Help me to know when to speak and when to remain silent
Help me nurture the talents
You've given me
and show me the gifts
I have been too blind to see
Teach me to live in this moment,
and not fret about the future
Tell me how
to shape the world in Your vision
Forgive me my past,
I have sinned on my way to You
And forgive those who sinned against me
Each breath is a gift
but also a prayer
When I dream, teach me
so I may enter another day
a better person
I want to live as You intended
And if it is Your will,
give me another tomorrow so I may ask this of You…
again

K. D. Kinz

Katie